D I L
deeply in Love
with yourself

NEENA PAUL

D I L deeply in Love with yourself
Copyright © 2019 by Sandeep Kaur

Tellwell Talent
www.tellwell.ca

ISBN
978-0-2288-2265-3 (Hardcover)
978-0-2288-1540-2 (Paperback)
978-0-2288-1541-9 (eBook)

Table of Contents

Note From The Author vii
Acknowledgements...xi

PART I

Let's Celebrate Life

Chapter 1   What Is Love?.....................................5
Chapter 2   Family 11
Chapter 3   Relationship With Relationships..........19

PART II

Realization

Chapter 4   Active And Passive.............................27
Chapter 5   Reason And Purpose...........................35
Chapter 6   Sympathy And Empathy.....................43
Chapter 7   Which And Where 49
Chapter 8   The Devil's Instinctive Mind...............59
Chapter 9   Good And Only Good 65

PART III

The New You

Chapter 10 Transmutation 77

Chapter 11 Intellect And Wisdom.........................83

Chapter 12 Detachment In Attachment 93

Chapter 13 The Super-Conscious Mind 101

Chapter 14 Affirmation 105

Chapter 15 Highest High And Lowest Low 115

Chapter 16 Success..121

Note From The Author

When I was growing up, I would often ask my mother, "What will be my path of life going forward?" I would always feel gratitude, and I had an attitude of appreciation and thankfulness for the benefits I had received.
She would just smile and say, "Dear, you will see your direction even before you start treading on it."

I would write small poems, which at times were even laughed at (in a good sense, though). This feeling of giving out to the world, of helping people in every possible way, made me work very hard during the prime years of my career. I held a very senior position in a security and management organization.

I would always look at the finalization of a contract or an assignment in terms of how many people would be employed, and how many mouths would be fed with one employment.

I have been a person of action, and not one of empty words or promises. It was not easy for me to take a down-to-earth approach in showing others how to empathize and care.

I always felt that my efforts could help other people achieve their goals, by being a hard worker and a team builder.

At times my sincerity led me into conflict with authority, because I'd rather fall on the sword doing the right thing than cave into the authority and do the wrong thing.

This desire for righteousness and helping others drew me towards damaged people because I felt the need to rescue them. Eventually, I made people jealous of my success to the point that they worked against me.

Then I realized what my mother had meant every time I asked her about my way to go. My natural empathy for others led me to find ways to deal with them with sensitivity, and this gave a new dimension to my existence.

I reached a point in life, when somehow, everything and everyone closest to me, just left me. All the awards, social recognition, and success were reduced to allegations and distress.

I finally understood the emptiness I had always felt throughout my life, despite all the fame, success, and grandeur I experienced. I was driven to search for something which I had never known. All this fame and social acclaim were meaningless.

Then I took my "Leap of Faith."

"REPLACE TEARS WITH PRAYER AND
FEARS WITH FAITH"
were the first lines I wrote.
Miracles happened!
With the outburst of all the emotions that I felt at this
junction, the only emotion that pulled me through was
the emotion of Love.
Love with the Creator, Love for the Creator, and Love
of the Creator.
Hence, I named this book *DIL* which in Hindi means
"heart." It is the heart which feels the love.
Love is an inside story.

This began my journey to feel and experience the
surrounding energies and ultimately merge with them.

Believe me, once you find the purpose of your life,
this journey itself becomes sweeter than honey, brighter
than the sun, and cooler than a cucumber. Then you
can even smile through your tears.

The more people I am able to meet, help, and share this
experience called "LIFE" by helping them define their
own, the more fulfilling my life becomes. To help others
find their purpose — that is the whole aim.

I feel that life becomes purposeful when you share
Unconditional Love.

After helping and guiding so many people in their lives, I realized that it was important for me to reach out to many people. No matter what age group, and no matter which part of the world they live, I dedicate my life in order to have them join me on this journey and form a bond.

"EACH ONE TEACH ONE."

Through sharing the life experiences of so many people, I have come to realize that this world is a beautiful place for each one of us.

As you read the book, you may find that you relate it to your own life experiences — that will be your starting point.

While I was still in the process of figuring out the contents of my book, a doctor at Apollo Hospital in Delhi, India, described the recovery process of a breast cancer patient.

In her testimonials, she mentioned the healing and guidance that I was giving to the cancer patient throughout the entire process, from diagnosis to chemo and finally total healing.

Today, people across the world are joining together to formalize this new path of self-realization and living life to the fullest.

Acknowledgements

Writing this book has been the best experience of my life. However, none of this would have been possible without all those people who doubted me, since their doubt was the firm foundation for me to explore the UN-explorable.

I would like to start by expressing my special appreciation for all those people across the globe who are mentoring others, especially the youth of today, since they are the ones taking the legacy forward.

This world is a much better place today because of teachers like them.

First and foremost, I would like to thank THE GURU (my teacher and guide) who blessed me, my thoughts, and my pen. He is leading the way by connecting me with the best people in this process.

To all the people I have had the opportunity to lead and be led by, to all those who have believed in and trusted my advice and guidance at every step in their lives, I thank you for being an inspiration to me, for making my meditations strong, and for encouraging me to help more and more people.

I would like to thank each and every person with whom I have interacted in my life, as each one has taught me something valuable. These people are the foundation for all my writings.

I am thankful for the life experiences I gathered during my years of professional success. For the support of my team members — you gave me the opportunity to lead a great group of individuals. To be a leader of great leaders is a blessed place to be. Thank you, everyone.

Living an experience, feeling it, experiencing it, and then writing about it has indeed been a life-changing experience both internally and externally.

I especially want to thank all those who helped me help them, to find themselves.

I would like to thank my parents, my brother, and my two sons. You are the ones who completely understand my craziness at all times.

I would like to thank Jennifer at Tellwell. That first phone call we shared gave me a feeling of joy that this dream was finally coming true. I would like to thank Caitlin for her help. I would also like to thank my editors and the marketing team for helping me reach out to every corner of the world, far and wide. To the production team, Joy as my Project Manager as well as Von and Joemar for designing the book.

… In gratitude…

PART I

Let's Celebrate Life

Spirituality and the divine, in today's world, seem like very impressive words coming from some "heaven" or outer space.

When the world talks about de-stressing, awareness, improving one's basic lifestyle, veganism, or calorie-counting, you are actually following the status trends of today.

The most fundamental element of the "individual" as a "Living Being" is completely ignored.

In the endeavor to simply bring to each and every individual across the entire world the reality of his or her own existence, I would like to talk about "Connectivity."

Oceans and mountains are crossed over simply with a phone call or an email, but this is connectivity with the outside world.

What about your own connectivity with your own self?

If I may ask a simple question — What are the things you like the most in this world?

You may name several things depending on your individual choices, but how long would it take you to name yourself?

This is the reality: we have not identified ourselves.

When you are engrossed in the day-to-day living, you are so much outwardly entangled that you often fail to even talk for a second with yourself.

Connecting with yourself in the early hours of the day or at any single moment of your day gives you energy for the entire day.

In this endeavor, Live Love Life brings you your time with yourself.

When a small child is thrown up in the air, the infant smiles upon seeing the safe hands ready to hold him in the blink of an eye. The tiny soul is in the air for seconds with a smile on his face because of his confidence in the parent. He has faith and trust in the hands of the face looking up at his smile.

When we come into this world, there is a "PARENT" SUPREME. We may call him/her by any name, but the "DIVINE" is ONE who holds the string (Dori) of our every breath.

Let's start out each day by seeking the blessings of that most powerful SOURCE which is much higher than the heights of life and death.

1

What Is Love?

The first emotion which God puts in all human beings in the entire universe is Love.

What is love?

Who put this love in human beings? Was this injected into the body, was it some kind of a bug that bit mankind, or is it a genetic disorder?

Those who do not believe in the word 'Love' would surely say that it is a genetic disorder because when you fall in love, your cheeks flush, your heart beats faster, and your head starts spinning. All this because of the chemical hormones that flood your brain and body.

This leaves you with feelings of euphoria similar to an endorphin-induced "runner's high."

Is love an emotion?

Is love a feeling?

Is love an epitome which the modern world uses today to build up one cell upon the other and then crash? Oh!! I was in love, but today there is a breakup… First you mix the ingredients, and then you bake a pie.

First, I want to know the ingredients before I bake this pie called Love.

Earlier there was love, and now it is over.

Does that mean that now the pie is overcooked and, in some cases, burned?

Or is that love is just an expression?

Oh, today I feel so loved; he brought me flowers. I feel so loved because she made me my favorite dinner.

I wish it was that simple.

He got her flowers because they were on a special: buy one get one free. She baked the best dinner because she had too many zucchinis growing in her back yard and they were just lying there rotting.

It's as simple as that.

Why do we mix love with gift items or gestures?

We shall talk about this in later chapters. At present, the question is where did this love come from?

Did it come from the baked or the burnt pie, or from the backyard organic vegetables, or where?

Interestingly, animals do not possess this same emotion {which I will call it for now}.

The lioness or the tigress who is supposed to be ruling the jungle and protecting her cubs (king or queen of the jungle) goes around the jungle nurturing and protecting her cubs and feeling proud as she watches them grow. The same is seen in ducks and other birds.

A birdie flies around in the early morning, gathering food for the new tiny life forms and then teaching them how to fly. In a pond, basking in the sun, the duck instructs the cutie ducklings to form a line behind her and swim.

Now no one has drawn any lines in the water, but those little tiny creatures know who makes them feel secure. And very timidly they follow the mother duck in a line. This has been one of the most fascinating sights for me.

So, if love means securing the little ones, then what happens when they grow up and are on their own? And if it is just about providing security for the little ones, then what about love for people of our age and the elderly?

When the grandfather puts a dollar bill in the hands of his granddaughter {because that's all he can afford from his monthly pension}, or the grandmother knits a beautiful woolen scarf for her granddaughter's graduation gift, is that love?

If love is an emotion, then is it the expression of our belongingness? Most of you would ask why do you need to define love?

Love is Love.

Then what is love?

In the monsoon season, the rain and the green trees are the same for everyone, and for those in love — romance is everywhere in the air.

For the one who has lost a loved one and is mourning, the same rain makes him depressed and lonely.

And for someone who has just had to fight... oh my God, the heavens have fallen. The heavens are crying as droplets of rain. In fact, the heavens never ever fall, but the pain that is felt is so excruciating that you feel that the strongest thing (the heavens) will fall.

Now it's the same rain, the same surroundings, the same you, and the same me, but what's different is how you look at it, how you feel it, and how you connect to it.

The connection that you share with your inner self when you see the rain expresses your inner emotions and how you are feeling at that point of time.

These different emotions express your mood, and what and how you are feeling at that given moment when the rain is falling.

The same rain is a smile for some and a tear for others, depending on how you are feeling within. It depends on the relationship you are having with your own self at that moment.

Now the question is who is going to determine our emotions — the weather, or the rain?

It's sunny, I'm happy; it's raining, I'm sad; it's cold, I'm miserable; it's hot, oh my God why did you make summer?

All your relationships are framed around this kind of mental preordained feeling.

So, let's come back to love. What is love and from where did this feeling come?

Love is an expression, an emotion, a feeling. It is exhibited by each one of us the moment we come into this world.

The first bonding, even before we come in human form, is felt in the womb. The mother gently touches her baby, and the emotions are felt.

Some scientists have gone to the extent to establish that the mother can teach children while they are still in the womb. But in the world of science there is no word for emotion, for any emotion of love, and so there's another conflict.

Interestingly, from birth to death this is the same main emotion that helps you grow and become who you want to be, no matter how many people come into your life as you grow.

Let me sum it up by saying that love is that feeling or emotion which is the foundation of our existence.

You do realize this emotion with the people around you, in your surroundings as you grow, and with all materialistic things that surround you. However, in this entire journey called life, you tend to fall apart without realizing this emotion within your own self. Take a moment and ask, "When was the last time I connected with myself?" When did you tell yourself that you love you?

It is you who gives birth to this emotion of love. It is you who has to love yourself in order to understand and share this emotion with the outside world.

*You can love people around you only if
you love your own self.*

TASKS

EVERY TASK SHOULD BE CONTINUED WITHOUT FAIL FOR AT LEAST THIRTEEN DAYS IN ORDER TO START SEEING VISIBLE CHANGES IN YOU.

1. Since the first emotion is love, every day, first thing in the morning, affirm to yourself that you love yourself. It should be simple, yet firm. Say, "I love myself the most."

2. No matter how much hatred or pain there is inside of you, and no matter if you are disappointed and disillusioned, you need to tell yourself that you love your own self.

3. At least thirteen times first thing in the morning, and again before you go to bed, repeat "I love myself." Remember that you need to love yourself and feel the gratitude towards your own self in order to start loving others.

Family

The first emotion that is felt when a human being is born is the emotion of love.

When a woman conceives, the first feeling shared by her and her child is an invisible bond, an unknown connection that we may define as love.

It is strange that as we grow old, we tend to forget and ignore that bond. The world around us, the organic, the contraptions, or the widgets fascinate us much more.

This bond of love — the first expression — is felt in the family.

So, what is a family?

There are several interpretations of family — nuclear family, joint family, extended family, single parent family, etc., but no one has explained what exactly is the meaning of family.

I would define family as follows:

Mother and Father, I love you.

It's as simple as that.

Mother and Father, I love you.

Since the first expression of love is felt with our parents, the parent is the mother giving birth and the second person after her who embraces the baby.

How conveniently we tend to move away from family for our outside worldly needs. *The Guru Granth Sahib* (The holy book of the Sikhs) clearly mentions "poota mata ki aasis, mata ki aasis," meaning born out of the blessings of the father and the mother. The Guru is the father and the mother because it's their bond (leaving aside the physicality part of it) which is responsible for the existence of a being.

Why is the mother's name said twice? "God could not be everywhere, thus he made mothers," as the popular saying goes.

Mother is not just for human beings. If you look at trees, a small branch or shrub grows out from its root. Now, in this case, the root is there, giving the tree unconditional nourishment for its survival.

More spiritually speaking, the embodiment of light or the flash of the first heartbeat which is felt in the womb is nothing but the grace and blessings of the Creator. In fact, the actual life that is being formed in the embryo is considered to be the blessing of the universe upon the mother. Have you ever wondered why a woman becomes a mother only when she gives birth (or adopts these days)?

Science may have succeeded in giving birth to the test tube baby, etc., but the first form of life that is put in the scientifically-grown embryo has remained a mystery for scientists even today.

Interestingly, it is imperative to mention here that the expression of love is felt by the mother (in most cases) when she gets to know that she's pregnant.

The emotional outburst of love starts in that very instant. It is important to mention here that experiencing the physicality of the baby in the womb occurs almost after the fifth month.

But love spurs from the words: "I am pregnant, wow..."

If the first expression of Love is felt at that moment when the womb is just as small as a cherry, then how does this bond become an epitome of love for the entire life of the individual and far beyond?

Mother, child, love stands as a benchmark of unconditional love. No matter how far away or close, no matter how many fights or misunderstandings occur between the two, this bond of Love is the first to make the newborn feel secure, and secure for life... Until the end of life... even after she's gone... as a guardian angel. Mom is still there... in fact, the bond of love created at the time of birth with the mother actually dies after the death of the child and even after the death of the children, and grand children.

They say unfortunate are those children who do not get the blessings of their mother, and it's true because she is one person in everyone's life who loves UNconditionally.

Loving unconditionally is a big term and important to understand if you have to understand love.

The first relationship is that of father and mother for any being who is born.

Typically, in families where there is superiority of the male child over the female child, the father would want a baby boy. The purpose of the boy would be to take over the business or work when his father grows old. The son will do this for his father. The son will complete his journey of life by giving him a flame so that his soul shall rest in peace.

If I may ask, do pictures of dead people speak?

Do they come and tell us that they are enjoying the world above, whatever that would be?

Then why do we have this condition attached to parental love by the father? His love for his son is conditional: "My son will do this when he grows up; my son will do that when he grows up; etc." But when it comes to the daughters… the irony is… she gets married and she goes away to her new home, so the level of acceptance of anything in return from the daughter is minimal, hence the taboo attached to the birth of a girl.

So, my question again is why are there conditions attached to love? Why do we have a benchmark or a scale for comparison? Why do we have an expectation?

The mother becomes a mother nine months before the father becomes a father. Those nine months are enough for her to feel that unconditional love towards the unborn child.

A mother would never say, "Wow, my son will look after me in my old age." She would, however, always say that "My child should get the best," and she would try and do whatever it takes, in every possible way, and strive her entire life to make sure she does the best for her children.

She will perhaps be the only person in the entire world who wants her child to outshine her, with a selfless motive, unlike the father.

I know that all the menfolk reading this would say, "No, this is not true," but I ask you a simple question…. when you see your son fighting or arguing on the streets with someone known or unknown, how many times have you taken a minute to sit with him and talk to him, a one-on-one man-to-man talk filled with a parent's advice?

When your daughter is bullied by her schoolmates, or when she is ready to go to prom night, how many times, not as a father but as her best guide or friend, have you talked with her for ten minutes?

How many times have you spent time with your son who is a little weak in his studies and who has not scored well in his exams? Have both of you discussed the possibilities of a poor performance?

I don't need answers; the answers are for your own self.

Conditions are attached to the bond of love between the father and his children.

There is unconditional love, even if Mom just has a few minutes to put her angel to bed, read a bedtime story, and give her blessings with a kiss on the forehead. She would not demand anything else in return.

That's unconditional love.

Now I certainly do not want to get into a gender equality debate here.

Unconditional love is simply a form of Selfless Love. This means a condition wherein one is giving without the least expectation or, anything in return, ever.

The question then is... does this kind of unconditional love exist in the world?

You can only love someone if you have felt this emotion towards your own self, and who is the person to teach you this? It is you, yourself. When you do not have any expectation from the person you love, this is called unconditional... there are no strings attached.

Unfortunately, our society today defines love with physicality. However, sex is not love; sex is sex.

Love then is an expression that gives you a feeling of belongingness to this world, a means of connection to the outside.

But what about our inside?

What about loving myself?

My question is...

When did you last love yourself?

TASKS

EVERY TASK SHOULD BE CONTINUED
WITHOUT FAIL FOR AT LEAST
THIRTEEN DAYS IN ORDER TO START
SEEING VISIBLE CHANGES IN YOU.

1. Since the first emotion is love, every day, first thing in the morning, affirm to yourself that you love yourself. It should be simple, yet firm.
2. Leaving your disappointments, pain, or hatred aside, you need to tell yourself that you love yourself.
3. Since the emotion of love is experienced through your parents, take a moment to hug your parents. Feel the love and be grateful to them for bringing you into this world.
4. Make a conscious effort to talk to them every day, even if it is just a short two-minute phone call.

Relationship With Relationships

Have you ever wondered why we are born alone (even if we are born as twins or triplets), and why we die alone?

Imagine for a moment when the child is born. With the exception of the mother's bosom, he doesn't know anyone at all.

Here, there is no relationship whatsoever which that infant has with any of the crowd called relations or acquaintances or people around him.

As the child grows, he is taught that this is your father, grandfather, grandmother, brother, sister, cousin, uncle.

Interestingly, in this modern world as we are moving more towards a robotic lifestyle where there's a 'one child' philosophy, we should be prepared to accept a lack of relationships in the generations to come.

So how, say after two decades, will we tell the child that this is your maternal uncle or your paternal aunt or your mother's sister's son, etc.?

Are we not moving too much towards the nuclear family? In this process of a new culturally restricted family style, how will we explain these relations after a few years? It will be even difficult to tell your child that he or she is your paternal cousin, since there will be nobody his/her age on the paternal side.

In this process of a small family, society is literally creating airtight compartments for the next generations where their interactions are more with gadgets and social media and less with real relations that he is born with.

By growing up with these relationships, the infant starts perceiving these relationships in a way that his/her own parents perceive their relationships.

This young lad is unconsciously influenced by the behavior patterns of the seniors around him.

For example, the mother's relationship with her mother-in-law is strained (which is the case in most modern households the world over), so typically the child is influenced likewise.

The father does not talk to the mother's brother, so the poor kid is strictly instructed not to talk to or interact with anyone in the mother's family.

Have you ever thought about what are you doing in this process?

You are trying to govern the relationship with the relationships your own children are growing into.

Unconsciously you also provide an environment to the growing young teenager where you show bias. You teach him/her how to be judgmental. You try to impose your own emotions with your relationships upon the child who is probably in a completely different state of mind to perceive and maintain the relationships in his or her own way.

Interestingly, I haven't heard any teenager say, "My father has told me not to talk to my maternal grandparents, but I make sure that I talk to them at least once every day, because my relationship with my grandparents is not dominated by the hatred or opinion of my parents."

I don't mean to say that I expect teenagers to disobey their fathers; nonetheless, what is important here is that you as parents need to ask, "Am I giving my children the freedom to have a relationship with the relationships they are born into this world, without any baggage of my own discretion and discrimination?"

If the father himself is teaching his own son a benchmark to govern his relationship with his grandparents with the same yardstick he uses to govern the relationship with his in-laws, then what do you expect that teenager to teach his own children after fifteen to twenty years?

Are you not imposing your own relationship to relationships upon your children?

Why can you not let them decide on their own if they want to talk to their grandparents or not?

On the one hand, you complain that your children don't respect you. On the other hand, you are the one teaching them consciously or unconsciously the art of being judgmental, not realizing that they are the new generation of kids who are moving away from valuable and deep relationships.

So, imagine a teenager who already has the pressure of academics, piano classes, soccer coaching, jazz classes, homework, and assignments, and then on top of that, you add the pressure of, "You are going to your mother's sister's house. I want you to behave. No talking about my new car or the vacation we are planning to take in the Christmas break. If I get the slightest hint that you have told, we will go for the vacation, but you will not go with us."

"Wow... a straight threat for a nice Christmas vacation... Am I a fool to tell them anything..."

You have just now taught the teenager the art of compartmentalizing a relationship.

From now on, he will be very conscious of keeping these relations separate. It is interesting to see that these things actually happen so unconsciously. At times, you don't even realize what you have done in the process.

This is just one example.

By the time the young lad is in his mid-twenties, he has made all the compartments for every relationship.

Imagine a boy who was born empty-handed, a blessed soul who came as an angel into this world. By the time he has lived just over two decades of his life (assuming that a lifespan is seven to eight decades), how will he treat relationships in the rest of his life?

Are you teaching them to have a relationship with relationships that they were born into, or are you influencing that relationship which should be independent of your relationships?

Are you encouraging them to be more connected with people that they are surrounded by, or are you digressing them away from the relationships?

You create your own web of relationships in this world.

People Come Into Your Life
For A Purpose... Either You
Teach Them Something... Or They
Teach You...

TASKS

EVERY TASK SHOULD BE CONTINUED WITHOUT FAIL FOR AT LEAST THIRTEEN DAYS IN ORDER TO START SEEING VISIBLE CHANGES IN YOU.

1. Tell yourself every day that you love yourself, and that you are grateful to be alive.
2. You are grateful to every part of your body. You can affirm each part by saying, for example, "I thank my legs for carrying my weight every day and not failing me. I thank my heart for pumping blood throughout my body and giving me life. I thank my eyes for making me see the beautiful world around me, etc."
3. It is very important to remember here that these tasks are working magic inside of you; hence, gratitude to each part of your physicality is very important.
4. You are grateful to your parents. Express this gratitude to your mother and father every day. It's important to continue these tasks for a minimum of thirteen days.
5. Express gratitude to your mother, since she held you for nine months upside-down in that ball of fire, and she gave you food and energy when you hadn't even opened your eyes.
6. You need to express gratitude to your siblings, friends, and co-workers who are defining the relationships around you.

PART II

Realization

Before going further, you must understand the importance of both the internal and external journey on this path called life.

The external journey is all about doing things, actions, which have consequences — good or bad. The internal journey is the one that bears fruit, and leads to a life of completion.

It is imperative to understand here that in the external journey of life, you interact with the world around you, as a social being. You make relations, learn, earn, and carry an 'ego.'

This ego, or self-respect, is a very important part of your day-to-day existence. You just cannot have anyone take you for granted. You have to be fair and righteous. For example, if you have put in sixty hours of work in the week, you should be paid for sixty hours: not less and not more.

There is no scope of humbleness, meaning that you need to fully know and understand your own limits of righteousness.

In this social interaction process, you may show some people down, or someone else might show you down. You have to be an honest professional in whatever you do, while you are doing it, with your head held high.

The traits are completely different for the internal journey.

In the internal journey of life, there is no room for 'ego.' This is a journey of total surrender. Total surrender is when you neither exaggerate nor elaborate.

Exaggeration will satisfy your ego and pride, and at times insult others. Elaborating things will bring in self-praise and raise your own false expectations, since everyone loves praise and followers.

On this path there is truth, in its most naked form; and honesty, no matter how bitter it is. It is what it is.

When you are honest in all its total nakedness, you come to a point of not hiding anything from your own self first.

This is not about the world; this is only about yourself. This section explains how to understand these two journeys. Try and balance them to the best of your ability.

Active And Passive

A common question I have been asked in my sessions is: "I don't see any changes in me but I feel good; how is that?"

You need to understand that just as in English language you have the active and passive voice, in our lives also it is the same. The ACTIVE GROWTH refers to the visible changes which individuals go through, meaning you change, your attitude changes, your code of conduct changes, your way of dealing with people changes, your voice changes, your body posture changes, your body odor changes, and you are more active now.

PASSIVE GROWTH occurs when internally you tend to start becoming more conscious of your existence. You have a smile on your face, and you start understanding that life is way more purposeful than just to whine and crib over small things. These changes are the result of your passive growth. You start looking for a purpose in life.

When you see yourself in the mirror you like what you see — but what you see is only the physicality. However, the changes that take place internally are the typical features which first and foremost only you can see. It is like when you do apply your makeup, you are the one who knows which shade of foundation to use. Internally, when you become more conscious of your existence, and of your mere presence itself, then you start witnessing changes in yourself. For example, you just start noticing your own eyes, your own voice.

It's something like saying that its the same old you in a new form.

This is the result of passive growth.

A simple example that will make it easy to understand is that the doctor treats you after seeing the symptoms in your physicality. He checks your pulse, checks your blood pressure, and diagnoses your ailment. He suggests some tests to be done and then the treatment follows. He does not straightaway ask you to lie down on the operating table and say, "I have to cut your sinus glands."

He gives you the symptomatic diagnosis and then he gives you the medicine accordingly.

In our lives, we work on both active and passive growth. All our lives, we are the only ones who can use the active vision of what we see to help us grow in our self-consciousness.

If passively we are advanced, then we have completed our journey to our super-subconsciousness and our awareness of it. Through discipline and meditation, you become aware of your being. You can use this passive strength to first help yourself in the active form. Then, you can help other people in their active form.

You need to understand here that your consciousness or your awareness of this internal movement will only start from the outside by observing things around you and by following patterns. Always remember that the universe or true nature and your surroundings is always giving you insight and direction. You need to understand and observe this. It's like reading between the lines.

It is as simple as saying that when you exercise, you plan and work towards your goal. You expect results the very first day you hit the gym. However, that does not happen. It is a process that you have to go through which not only involves an exercise plan but also healthy eating habits and some lifestyle-changing choices. The exercise is the active part of the change, whereas the eating, the sleeping, and the lifestyle changes are the passive part of the change.

The results are not instant. The first few observations become visible often after about two weeks of regular exercise and eating healthy. So basically, what you're trying to do is release the active and the passive for your own physicality to improve your lifestyle.

Let us put the same example in the journey that we are discussing here.

Actively, it is your consciousness, your present moment in life and your belongingness in this world which connect you to your surroundings in terms of what you see and observe in people around you. This can be referred to here as the exercise routine. Passively, it is your consciousness. You are your internal self which is making you understand the phenomenon of the things and patterns around you. You need to understand this, just like you need to eat healthy.

When you look at both the active and passive in collectivity, they form a process wherein the results are obvious and visible to the world. After three weeks of exercise and healthy eating, you will not only feel good physically (that is actively), but it is possible that you will feel happier internally. You will feel more at peace with yourself.

In the journey of consciousness, once you become passively active, you are in a position to not only change and regulate your own lifestyle, but you are also able to encourage people around you. People around you will start to notice these changes. You will also become more desirous to know about the cause and effect of the force behind these changes in your own self, just as you would like to ask a very healthy and fit person at the gym to share their workout routine.

It is imperative to mention here that if passively you are more active, meaning that your level of consciousness is much higher than your understanding, then internally your body will react by deciding to eat healthy or have a particular kind of a lifestyle. For example, one fine day you will wake up and decide to start taking yoga classes. One fine day you will say that you don't want to eat non-vegetarian because your body does not accept meat anymore. This could happen to anyone at any stage of their life. You need to be aware of observing these indications coming to you from the universe or your own self because you are an integral part of the universe. Once you are aware of how to manage your active and passive life, you are brought to the next stage of awareness wherein you not only understand the meaning of cleansing yourself internally but you are also aware of the active acts and deeds you need to do.

It is very important to understand that both these journeys, the active outside worldly visible one and passive internal one, go side by side throughout our life.

Even if both these journeys go simultaneously in your lives, the awareness in understanding both may not happen together. You may tend to observe your passive growth more than your active growth, making you feel a more evolved soul from inside. On the other hand, you may feel a strong urge for discipline in your active lifestyle and may not be as aware of your own evolution.

Having said that, once you become aware of both your active and passive sides, this becomes a game changer. Now you need to learn how to balance both of your journeys in order to come to a point of total balance. Both become visible outwardly and inwardly.

These journeys are like train tracks running parallel throughout your life. It is your constant endeavor to make them converge into one so that both active and passive become one single form. This will then take you to a higher level of consciousness where you are not only internally aware of your existence, but you could also help others on the same path.

No One Knows You Better Than You Know Yourself... Be Honest To Yourself.

EVERY TASK SHOULD BE CONTINUED WITHOUT FAIL FOR AT LEAST THIRTEEN DAYS IN ORDER TO START SEEING VISIBLE CHANGES IN YOU.

1. By now you should have started feeling some kind of a relief or relaxation with a lighter feeling inside of you.
2. Continue your tasks from Part I.
3. Start recognizing with each expression of gratitude to yourself and your kin the feeling of belongingness.
4. Your feeling of gratitude to yourself should become firm now.
5. Your inner self expresses gratitude to your body.
6. Increase the number of times you say "I love myself" to yourself to more than twenty times each day.
7. After you eat, express gratitude to your senses, tongue, teeth, and digestive system to help you experience the pleasure of food.
8. After walking, express gratitude to your legs for taking you through.

You should start seeing changes in yourself. The first indication would be that you will start living a happier and more fulfilling life each day.

Reason And Purpose

Once this consciousness starts developing, it gives direction to a new you. You start seeing the changes within your own self. At this time, an array of questions will arise in your inquisitive mind. You will automatically start realizing that you are no longer sitting and chilling with the old friends of yours, who no matter how good they are, their weather talk, discussions, and jokes are actually meaningless. You start looking for people to associate with who are actually like-minded and on a similar path as you are.

For example, when you start exercising, during the first week it is very difficult for you to exercise alone. However, when you have an exercise partner, not only does your workout become more interesting, but you also start becoming aware of eating healthy and moving towards a better lifestyle. It is very strange in your life that you tend to do things to relate to or impress other people around you. You look at what they are doing. For example, if your exercise buddy does ten push-ups, then you would like to do twelve. You tend to challenge yourself in order to get out your optimum self. Guess what the result is: a better you today, than yesterday.

This awareness inside of you actually opens new horizons of thought, processing, and knowledge which then lead you to associate with like-minded people. You start reading and trying to look more for questions and answers because these questions and answers are actually arising from within your consciousness. Suddenly, you will find yourself eating healthy and looking at the ingredients. You will also start observing your neighborhood surroundings. You will want to be associated more with nature and your surroundings.

These changes are happening because you are now transitioning into a position of understanding the purpose of your existence in this universe. The universe at this stage gives you indications of why you are there. I often have people asking questions such as why was I born? What am I supposed to do? How am I supposed to find out what my life should be? How am I supposed to know where I go? These questions arise in your mind only when you become a searcher. Then, you start searching. You start singing to the realities of life; you start becoming more inquisitive. You start becoming more aware of your own existence. What makes you aware of your own existence is actually your surroundings.

You will always feel that when you eat clean, you live clean, you like clean, you feel clean, and your thoughts are cleaner than they were before. This cleansing process as mentioned earlier not only actively or passively teaches you, but it also puts you on the right path. When I say right, I mean a more conscious path. Now you are not only aware of all your actions, but you are consciously aware of the consequences of your actions. So, you just don't do things. First, you are consciously aware of its result; and then, you do the action.

I feel that life is a journey of the individual to discover his own self. When you go on the path of discovering yourself, you have to discover yourself using the objects, findings, and means given to you. A two-year-old in a pool who tries to learn swimming does not put his nose in the water to start getting the feeling of drowning. He does not start by moving his legs and feet to learn swimming. Instead, his natural instinct is to flip flap his legs and arms in order to stay afloat. It is a very interesting sight to see a toddler learn how to swim. It is as if he is in a self-discovery mode. And that is exactly what this life is: a self-discovery mode for each one of us. On this journey called life it is important for you to start observing the small things around you. Everything around you is giving you a story; you need to understand the clues.

As they say… the best things in life often come in small packages…

Once you are in that position, you will feel that there is a very thin, curtain-like film which has broken. Once the curtain is removed, you will start looking at all the things which you were singing about earlier with the same eyes but a different you. For example, you may look at the same trees in the same garden that you have been walking in for the past fifteen years. Or you may look at the same snow-covered mountains in front of you. But this time, it is a different you. You try to see the beauty behind the flowers, which earlier you were not even aware of.

Welcome... this is the new you... you have discovered... who was always there inside of you, though you were unaware.

And this is when I say repeatedly the more you talk to yourself, the more you will feel connected. The more you talk to your own self, the more you will make your own self understand what is happening within you and around you. Observe what you see around you. The more you connect with the universe, the more you will understand the true meaning of life.

Now what does this indicate? It simply indicates a shift of your own paradigm from the reason why you were born to the purpose of your life. It may sound like a very small paradigm shift, but it is actually a life-changer. Because once you move from the stage of reason to the stage of purpose, the whole ideology changes.

Now you have become a Seeker. Now you want to understand. You ask the universe the purpose of your existence. Is your purpose only to pay the bills every month, raise a family, and then die? Or is there a bigger purpose? Do you take the responsibility to give something back to the universe at large, or to your source of existence from where you were given this life form? Is your purpose of life to help others?

It becomes very fascinating when you have the paradigm shift from reason to purpose. You suddenly start associating with people who have a similar purpose as you do in your life. You start understanding their purpose and how they are trying to fulfill this purpose, as they go forward in terms of understanding what nature is teaching them.

Now this new DESIRE in you to reach out to people, a feeling of giving to the universe, is actually a DESPERATE FIRE inside of you making you experience this paradigm shift.

Let us look at this newfound desire. It is like the light that you see before entering a tunnel. You only see the light that is required at that point in time. The indications which the universe gives you change in terms of your own physical surroundings. You only need to see the next few steps; you do not see the end of the tunnel. It is important for everyone, no matter which country, area city, or direction you're coming from, to get into the tunnel. Understand that the process of seeking enlightenment is the same the world over (hence, the tunnel is the same for everyone). You have to come to a point of understanding your own self, with the help of taking small steps, in order to solve the mysteries as challenges that your life gives you. Every time you solve one problem in your life, the mystery of your journey gives you clarity towards the next step. In the process your own purpose starts becoming clearer.

The discovery of this new you will make your thoughts and your actions become completely focused on a different "purpose" of your life. Now you will not just do things out of the blue, but your actions will be more meaningful. You will start associating yourself with like-minded people.

Once you enter this tunnel of enlightenment, the universal energies around you start showing you the path forward. For example, out of nowhere you may get an invitation for a free week of yoga classes. Or you will meet some stranger and he would start talking about his journey, and you will get answers to what was going on in your mind.

Then you will start making new friends, mainly those who have experienced what you are going through right now in your life or who are experiencing the same. You will start adapting to a new, more disciplined lifestyle.

At this stage you will start feeling that you do not have the desire to do certain things. For example, if you were a smoker, you may not feel the urge to smoke. Or you will just want to eat turkey instead of beef. It can be as simple as not going out for a volleyball game. Instead, you will sit in your back yard and read. There can also be drastic changes in your lifestyle. For example, you may feel the desire to meditate.

As mentioned earlier, starting up practices such as yoga, exercising, nature walks, long trail walks, sitting under trees, sitting by the lake, and just watching the sunset are some of the signs that will tell you that you are now coming to a paradigm shift within your own self. This is the stage when you will tend to become more sensitive, more vulnerable, more emotional, and more inquisitive because now you want to understand the purpose behind everything. This would actually leave you in a state of understanding the difference between sympathy and empathy.

Success has no boundaries.

TASKS

EVERY TASK SHOULD BE CONTINUED WITHOUT FAIL FOR AT LEAST THIRTEEN DAYS IN ORDER TO START SEEING VISIBLE CHANGES IN YOU.

1. I love myself.
2. I love every specific part of my body.
3. I love my father and mother. I love my mother.
4. I am grateful to my body for giving me an experience of this life.
5. I am in gratitude to my parents, my siblings (you can use specific names), my friends, and my colleagues.
6. I am in gratitude for being alive. (This becomes a very important task now since you are experiencing a feeling of connectivity to yourself.)
7. I am in gratitude to the world at large.
8. I am connected to the world around me. (This task should be repeated at least twenty-five to thirty times every day.)

Sympathy And Empathy

This is a new you who now understands the difference between reason and purpose. You are looking for a purpose. You are more conscious of your existence. You have become more sensitive towards your surroundings. The sensibility of identifying with similar people becomes obvious. You are more aware of your fellow beings.

You have become a SEEKER.

Now, recall instances in your life when you were confused, or when you met people on this journey of life and you felt they were weird. Today, you are in that position. You are at a higher-level. Earlier, when you would go to a social gathering you would actually say that a person was insane, probably because he was more lost in his own self. Actually, he was still trying to discover his purpose. He was still struggling to move from the window of reason to purpose; and hence, he was lost. Today, you will try and relate to him. Today, you can understand his sensitivities and find reasons why, when he watches a movie, he starts crying.

He is relating to something else in that movie which others are not able to see.

Before, when someone experienced an insight and explained the beautiful meaning of nature in his or her own words, you would laugh, saying, "Oh my God, this person has gone crazy." If you saw someone having tears in his eyes upon seeing some natural beauty you would not be in a position to understand. But now, when you relate or connect to the same scenery or beautiful environment, you also have tears in your eyes. You can relate to how that person was feeling at that point of time. You are resonating at the same level of consciousness as the other person.

Let me explain this with a simple example. Grade three children will always share their lunch breaks with grade three children; high school children will always share tiffin with their own classmates. You will not find a grade three child sitting and sharing a meal with a grade twelve child, not even if they are brother and sister. Soul children of a similar age group like to be friends with their own age group of like-minded fellow beings. Their souls are resonating at the same age in terms of maturity. For example, an eighty-year-old man may be best pals with a twenty-year-old young lad. Here their association and this intense bond of unconditional love is not in terms of the physicality; however, they might have been soul siblings in some of their previous lives. The bond can be so strong that at times, even without any physical interaction, they may be in two different parts of the world yet they can come together and become one.

Hence, you will start feeling that your soul is searching for people around you who are at the same level in this journey of the soul as you are.

It is strange that some of your associates or friends will become so distant that you will not want to meet them. You will have a completely different set of friends now because you are today at a different level in terms of the evolution of your consciousness. You are resonating at a higher level of consciousness compared to them.

This new sensitivity that you feel around you, as you relate to people in a completely different manner, is not sympathy. Instead, it is the result of your paradigm shift in becoming more sensitive towards coexistence in general. For example, before, if you had gone for a walk and you saw someone with their dog, you would have probably ignored them. But now, you actually stop for a second and say hello, not only to the person but also to the dog. It's not that you have suddenly become pet-friendly, rather you have become more sensitive to the mere existence of everything and every being around you.

Another simple example would be walking out of a subway station and seeing a doorman standing there with a box in his hand for a tip. With hundreds of people walking out of that subway station every single day, not everyone will stop and drop a penny in his box. In fact, the majority will actually ignore that he is even standing there because they do not even see him standing there. They are so involved in their own wrath of lies that they are just not sensitive to any coexistence. But there will be one sensitive person who drops a penny into his box. On days when this sensitive person does not have a penny to drop into his box, he will give the doorman a smile and acknowledge him with a hello. Now, this is not sympathy. This is empathy. It is your soul calling; it is your awareness and consciousness on this journey which is making you realize that you need to understand the sensitivity of the other person. The penny that you give to that person is not really important. The monetary value is insignificant to you. It is actually that moment or fraction of a second of your soul calling to his soul.

This journey called life is actually nothing but the journey of the soul. The physicality of the body is like the clothes that we wear to cover the soul.

Soul calling is like a chain. The soul attracts a soul. That is why when you meet someone out of the blue, you feel that you have already known this person for a long time. Can you start feeling that you have known people from before? The answer is Yes. You have never met this person, and suddenly you feel so attracted or associated and connected to the person. Basically, the souls that knew each other in past lives want to be together. You would have played an important part in their journey or they played an important part in yours. You need to understand and be aware of this fact. As I mentioned earlier, people do come into our lives for a reason or a purpose: either we teach them something or they teach us something. It is important to understand why we are meeting someone in particular in our life.

There are no coincidences.

TASKS

EVERY TASK SHOULD BE CONTINUED WITHOUT FAIL FOR AT LEAST THIRTEEN DAYS IN ORDER TO START SEEING VISIBLE CHANGES IN YOU.

1. All tasks from 1-8 as explained on pages 42-43.
2. Every single day, be conscious of saying thank you to at least one person.
3. Begin with your wife, husband, son, daughter, and colleague.
4. Add at least one more "I love you." Be careful here about choosing who you start saying this to. It may not be important for you to mention to a stranger that "I love you." Instead, you can mention "I love the way you drove the bus today," or "I appreciate that you cleaned the garbage from the pantry."
5. This is very, very important: you must consciously express gratitude to at least one person outside of your circle every single day.
6. If you remember just before going to bed that you have not expressed your gratitude to one person today, then pick up your phone and call your friend and tell him that you appreciate his support in your life. (Now it should not happen every day that you forget to express gratitude to even one single person in your entire day.)

Which And Where

Now comes the question: "How do I balance this outside world to which I belong with the inner world where I belong as well?"

See the difference — outside — is to which we belong, and — inside — is where you belong.

This journey from which to where is a mythical one. It would have been transcending for months, for years, for a lifetime, or for many lifetimes; who knows? But never forget that it is only in the human life that you have the only conscious opportunity to understand and connect with the light — source — core — your own self.

Now the question is: "Does that mean that animals, birds, and other beings that we see do not have a chance to be one with the One?"

For some animals, birds, and trees (for example, those who have a lifespan of over hundreds or thousands of years), imagine how much would they be struggling to find the purpose of their lives. They don't have this human form to actually merge with the Creator and spread the positivity around them. Have you ever noticed there are so many trees on the mountains, so many life forms living in the mountains, but can those trees say that they feel blessed having understood their purpose of life?

In fact, the mountains stand as the epitome of strength. The next time you go through the mountains, don't just see them standing there as big pieces of rock. Instead, try and see the strength they exhibit. They are relentless, unaffected by any kind of storm, and powerful in their determination to be standing there. Do not forget that they have been there for thousands of years.

Some of the birds or animal species may perhaps be much more evolved than most of the human species walking off the streets of Manhattan, but they do not have the consciousness of describing their journey like we human beings can do.

I would like to share some most unbelievable memories about some of the world's best places that have the best scenic beauty.

The moment you google exotic destinations in the world, you are shown the ten or twelve most beautiful and breathtaking seas, beaches, skies, mountains, cliffs, skylines, etc., but have you ever wondered what makes them so exotic?

Nature is at its best the moment you see that sunset on the beach. From the cliff, the beautiful snow-clad mountains with the sunshine literally bathing the peaks just take your breath away. At that moment there is a feeling of Wow, how beautiful is nature.

My question to you is: What is that wow — speechless feeling at that moment?

The answer is simple: The wow is what your eyes see, the freshness is what your nose smells, the gentle sounds are the waves you hear with your ears. You are sensing the stillness of the cold, chilly wind on the snow-covered mountain which seems to be whispering its own language, and your entire body experiences a different touch or a different flow of energy which perhaps you have never experienced before.

This is the wow.

The wow is a feeling generated by our own senses, our own body, and our own experience. The wow is the fact that you have very consciously taken a flight, bought tickets, booked the hotel, perhaps had a glass or two of the best scotch or vintage wine, and consciously arrived to experience this particular mesmerizing view of nature.

All your senses, your physicality, and your outer being trying to connect to one view of nature which, believe you me, is actually a phenomenon existing at that particular place every single day, year after year... every single day of the year.

This view is relentless, unchanged, and unaltered for years, but for you, that moment is priceless; it is a once in a lifetime experience.

The answer is simple.

For that particular moment in time, you connect with the world in "which" you are to the world "where" you belong.

That moment connects you to that innermost layer of super-subconsciousness in which you don't even realize that you are connected with your innermost self. It is a multi-million-millimeter fraction of a second when your entire senses come together to converge into that "where."

Now if I may say that at that pleasurable moment, or that micro moment of the second that you experienced, this connectivity with your innermost self can actually be a lifetime experience for every day, in every moment that you live.

You might think that I'm crazy.

But the fact is that this is true and simple. All we need to do is understand that we are living in the world "where" we are. Our day-to-day life with nature around us should actually help us connect ourselves to the world "where" we actually belong.

The world is just in an energy form. We are also a part of this energy movement, as are the fish and the whales in the ocean, the volcanos on the land, and the birds in the sky. All these are energy forms of the world "where" you belong.

The "which" is actually a "witch."

This "which" of the world has all the questions, and the "where" of the world has all the answers.

Strange, isn't it, that the paradigm may be so simple yet so explicit?

I have had people come and tell me, "Oh, I feel so good becoming vegetarian. I feel so good now that I haven't smoked for the entire week. I feel so light every night when I have my dinner at six. I feel so fresh when I go for a walk in the park."

All I give them is a sweet smile.

What have they done that gives them this sudden-found happiness? They have got a little bit of the which replaced by where. It is just a simple feeling of that elementary connection when all the actinic forces of the body are in the process of connecting with Mother Nature around them. This process has pushed the consciousness into the subconscious zone and the subconscious into the super-subconscious zone. But this is so momentary and happens in such a subtle way that what you feel is a feeling of being light, as if the body has been suddenly cleansed of all the muck it had stuck to it.

This process has to begin somewhere. Now, for many, this process gets attributed to their newfound habits with no understanding that every slight change in these simple habits is like the unfolding of petals on a lotus flower. Most of the people in today's modern world love yoga — oh, they start to feel that they have accomplished a newfound energy and a feeling of lightheadedness, like the "wow" they saw at the sunset. They are relating to that feeling here because once again, by changing some habits and lifestyle, they are trying to get all their cognitive forces to merge into their own being — hence, the feeling of lightheadedness.

But trust me, this feeling is just a green leaf of the beautiful lotus flower. There is no way you are near the blossom yet.

The transition from the outside world of "which" to the inside world "where" you belong isn't that easy.

It is the change of the dynamics, or the change of the dimensions, wherein instead of seeing the world only in the three dimensions that mathematics teaches you, you move into an experience of a different dimension to the extent of even going as far as up to 15 16 17 dimensions to what you see and experience. Once you come to a position wherein you have raised your existing and resonating frequency in terms of your own energy externally, perhaps there may not be many visible changes, but internally you start feeling as if something has changed, as if you are wearing a new pair of prescription glasses.

Experience is bliss, and this experience may be different for different individuals depending on their own evolution or the place where they are in their own journey.

With the first few experiences, you may not even realize that this was an experience, that you felt differently, perhaps simply at peace with yourself, lighter, or happier once you felt you reached your inner consciousness. The point here is to be aware of you. This is why I always suggest that you need to talk more to yourself. Observe what is around you; be very alive in every moment of your life. You never know what kind of message the universe through any natural phenomenon or an experience around you conveys to you.

Once you get to understand these experiences, your Karma's desire to know more and understand more is unleashed. It becomes a passion.

This passion, when developed, becomes purpose; and this purpose, when understood, becomes passion again. But this time this passion gives a different feeling, a different source of energy, a different feeling of fulfillment, since now it is coming from within you. Here the movement is inside out, not outside in.

As mentioned in the earlier chapters, when you realize this release, it is most likely that no one around you will understand you. This is not because you have transformed into a crazy being but because they are not yet evolving the way you are. They may not be resonating on the same frequency as you.

Let me emphasize here that it is okay if people around you do not understand you. At this moment, even you do not understand yourself. You are feeling the changes internally but are not able to break the code, simply because this is the first time such a thing has happened to you.

It is very important to understand that you are absolutely fine. You don't need to see a doctor when you just start crying randomly.

Interestingly, one of the typical symptoms of being in this position is depression. Here depression is not because of a mental state; it is mainly because of your own quest to search for the changes happening inside of you. You may feel frustration when you don't find answers, and you may feel more frustration when people around you do not understand.

Just remember that it is fine to be in this state. It is probably the universe telling you that you now need to raise your vibration. You need to intensify your internal cleansing by either meditating more often or connecting more within yourself. Connect more internally to your own self.

Then, when you quietly understand, everyone around you wonders. They do not understand the changes in you. When you make this understanding a message to be passed on with conviction, it becomes passion.

This passion comes from "where" you belong. Because you are here, you experience the bliss. Now you want to share and convey this bliss, this feeling of wow, just as after your exotic vacation you want to share the pictures and videos with your friends on Facebook or WhatsApp and make people envious of your vacation.

Here, it is the passion to convey that feeling to the world, so typically now we are talking inside out.

Moving from the super-super-consciousness to the super-consciousness and then to our own consciousness gives our mind the acceptance of a feeling, an awareness of a new source of new energy, and a different outlook to what we see around us.

Once in the outer domain of the lobe of realization, it becomes easier to transmit your awakening to the outside world.

Through your talk, walk, expression, body odor, or language, even if you do not want to speak, your awakened state will still be visible to those who have to see it, to those who do not have to connect, or to those who are not yet at that level of connectivity and consciousness to even understand or acknowledge.

Let me put it in a very simple way: when you were children, you read about Pythagoras' Theorem. Now, just as you read this sentence, the formula comes in your mind and you relate to it instantly. Your brain instantly registers with the word and instantly gives you the Pythagoras Theorem since you related to it. For some, it will be, "Yes, I know I read it when I was a child, but I don't remember it right now." For others, it will be, "I have heard the term but I'm not too sure about it."

In the same way, those who want to see these changes in you relate to you, resonate with you, and are on the same journey and probably at the same level as you. They will, no matter what, understand your position and every word you are saying, because somewhere down the line they too are experiencing or have experienced a similar kind of a surge of energy flowing from within their subconsciousness to their consciousness.

Life Is A Journey From Source Energy To Source Energy To Merge Back Into The Source Energy.

TASKS

**EVERY TASK SHOULD BE CONTINUED
WITHOUT FAIL FOR AT LEAST
THIRTEEN DAYS IN ORDER TO START
SEEING VISIBLE CHANGES IN YOU.**

1. All tasks from 1-8 as explained on pages 42-43.
2. All tasks on pages 28-29.
3. The most important part of your journey is starting now.
4. Start observing your surroundings. Express gratitude to the air you breathe, to the sun shining every single day, and to the moon giving light in the dark night.
5. Express gratitude to the sun for light.
6. Watch the trees or flowers on your way home and express gratitude to them for helping you breathe fresh air.
7. Feel the pleasure in the Wow moment around you every single day.
8. Search the internet for at least one beautiful place in the world every day and try and enjoy the beauty of nature.
9. Feel the fresh air in every breath you take.

The Devil's Instinctive Mind

Not every person on the Earth experiences or goes through these changes. These changes are not external changes; they are changes within the person. Your personality actually gets shaped in a different way when you become a Seeker.

Now it is important to understand that becoming a Seeker also means going on the path of enlightenment. Though this sounds intense, it does not happen overnight. You have to fight your own inner self — the dirty devil that also exists inside of you.

The devil may not necessarily provide intense opposition all the time; it could be the debate of any scientific explanation or any conflict or difference of opinion within your own mind. One very typical feature of a Seeker is that he is very argumentative. These arguments may not necessarily be so much with the outside world but more within his own self, and by getting these answers, he becomes a SEEKER.

Suddenly he becomes very inquisitive about all of his surroundings; he wants to know the answers to all the things that are happening. He starts to google everything; he wants to get knowledge about every little thing. Overnight, he wants to become a very aware and knowledgeable person.

This is the main reason why I mentioned earlier that you need to talk to yourself. The more you talk, the more you become aware that something is happening inside of you. The more you talk to your own self, the more you relate to yourself and find the answers. It is not so much a journey on the outside; it is more a journey on the inside.

The devil is actually like your pet dog. Now, if you don't give him food or take him out for a walk, he will retaliate since he does need his own social time. In the same way, the devil inside also needs to be active and has its own needs — making you do wrong things, speak wrong words, hurt people, and react to situations. Take a moment now and recall how many times you have had the devil overpower you and say some things to the one you love. Later, you regret having said those things.

My point exactly — take a moment to handle each experience. Each experience brings with it some reason. Each experience that you are having is now teaching you some methods to control the devil within you.

Earlier you would just react to anything said or anything that you felt was wrong. Your reaction to the action (of someone saying something wrong) would be so spontaneous that you would not even realize the consequence of your action.

Earlier, your reaction to your own action would create a dispute.

However, now you do not have any reaction for your own action (in terms of replying to the argument, etc.). Now, you just tend to ignore or stay silent as you don't feel the need to react.

Reaction is when you act on someone else's action. But now you have evolved to a point wherein you do not feel the need to react at all.

If the action is negative in the first place, then how do you expect the reaction to be positive? Thus, the devil overpowers and gives its action. Ultimately, the reaction to the negative will be more negative than the negative action itself.

Whenever you are in a situation like this, I know you have noticed that you have your inner voice giving you one option and the devil giving you another. Usually people tend to take the opinion that the devil suggests, and the consequence is that you have to experience another roller coaster of events that follow that negative reaction to the negative action in the first place.

When I say take a moment, I'm actually suggesting that perhaps you may become aware of that inner voice and you may listen to it. Or instead of the reaction to the action, just stay quiet, just forgive, or just smile.

Once you have done this, you will see how positive and good you feel for yourself. It's not just one stand-alone time that you have to fight the devil within and become victorious; there will be a series of such experiences in your life before you even become aware that you have the devil under your control. It is a repeated process unless you come to a point of taming the devil inside of you like your own pet dog.

Now you are the master and the devil will always listen to you.

Interestingly, the way to handle this devil within is not taught to us by anyone. It comes from the sub-consciousness and is guided by the super-subconsciousness, which actually comes to your consciousness as you become aware of it. The super-subconscious is your core, the innermost part of your being. It is the closest to your soul. Once you reach your super-subconsciousness, it sends a signal to your subconsciousness which in turn sends a signal to your consciousness. Understand that you are always living in your consciousness, the then and now.

The journey of enlightenment is reaching and connecting to your super-subconsciousness and living every second of your life totally connected.

Like I said earlier, more soul-searching experiences help you to relate to the outside world as you connect more to your own self.

On the outside journey you become more mature and experienced, and on the inward journey you go more inward as you come closer to the merging of the energy. The purpose of existence now is getting more defined. You are evolving.

The entire life process actually is to understand the inner process of evolving your consciousness and making you feel alive in every moment and every breath you take. This movement of your consciousness towards your super-subconsciousness is the internal process; however, you start feeling this movement externally in your own life as you evolve.

As a human, you should not try and determine your worth in others – you find your worth in yourself and for yourself.

TASKS

EVERY TASK SHOULD BE CONTINUED WITHOUT FAIL FOR AT LEAST THIRTEEN DAYS IN ORDER TO START SEEING VISIBLE CHANGES IN YOU.

1. All tasks from 1-8 as explained on pages 42-43.
2. All tasks on pages 28-29.
3. The most important task now is NOT TO GIVE UP.
4. REPEAT, REPEAT, AND REPEAT.
5. You should not fail now.
6. You have come this far. Connect with the universe, and do not fail yourself.
7. Remember that even if you fail for one single day in doing all the tasks, you will need to start all over again from day one.
8. I suggest keeping a journal. Mark day one and day twenty-one. If you successfully complete twenty-one days, do not stop. Start again, and again. Just as life is an ongoing process, living in gratitude and loving yourself is also an ongoing process.
9. DO NOT LET ANYTHING STOP YOU NOW.

Good And Only Good

Every experience is good — in fact the best — as each experience is your own evolution.

The very fact that you have come this far reading my book means that you have had experiences, fallen, risen, fallen, risen again, and come to the point of understanding that there is a reason why things happen. You will now start looking at that reason as a purpose, as discussed earlier.

Once you reach the stage of purpose, you will see that you can start finding something positive in everything that happens to you. Every experience teaches you something, helps in your own evolution as a human being, and goes deeper inside to merge with the self within you. It raises your consciousness. This experience is actually not an outwardly experience; it's the experience of the soul. It's the journey of the soul.

It's like when you play Monopoly. You have to make sure you have money and assets and yet return safely to your original home where you started to roll the dice. No matter the journey, and no matter what path you take, you still have to go through your roller coaster ride ensuring you will come back safe and sound to your house. Here, your house means coming one with your own consciousness. That is this journey called life. The kinds of experiences that you go through are actually evolving you to come in and merge with your innermost self.

You start crossing the barriers. You move from the conscious to the subconscious and then the super-subconscious until you come to the extreme — your own self. This is the being who you are. Once you have touched your innermost core of super-subconsciousness, it sends you a message which actually reaches your consciousness and makes you aware of your own existence. You start becoming aware of your consciousness. This entire process will probably take a fraction of a micro mini-second, but the evolution will take days and years and months as you evolve in this journey.

Similarly, this experience, or for that matter all your experiences, are meant to make you more mature and move you more inward within your own self. On this journey called life, going deeper can bring you to a point wherein you become one with your inside. Your soul connects to the universe and to that superpower all around you.

This is the main purpose of the existence of every living being in the universe: to merge yourself in with the Creator and become One.

Now, when you start enjoying nature in a different way, it's mainly this state of evolution of your inner consciousness when your inner soul gets connected with the natural existence around you.

In earlier chapters, I explain the feeling of exuberance and utmost bliss and excitement when you see something in nature. This is the feeling you start to live with now that you have evolved.

Being evolved here would mean that your innermost self closest to your soul gets connected to your surroundings and the universe. You start resonating energy. In fact, the physical body at this point is only a small part of the big energy ball around you.

That is why the Wow - that point of utmost connectivity and resonating higher energy through your consciousness — is so important.

Once you start to believe that whatever happens to you is only for your good, you start looking for positive in that challenge itself.

Then, what is bad is actually good Karma. It is good and only good. What tragedy are you actually experiencing? Then why stress to find a reason behind it?

This experience actually has a purpose.

This good will become best as you will learn from the experience. Face it, experience it, control your devil in the process, and find your purpose.

Literally everything is within you.

There are layers and layers from the conscious to the subconscious to the super-subconscious and to the innermost core where you have to reach in order to merge within.

Now in order to reach this awakened state, this self-God, your soul, your core, energy, or source, whatever you may call it, is within you. As a seeker you have to work every day of your life in order to attain this state of dwelling within your own consciousness yet totally connected with the universe at large.

Shapeless, beyond boundaries, beyond desires — just a ball of energy waiting for you to come and merge in.

The purpose for those who are lucky enough to read, seek enlightenment, and merge with their soul is to start the reverse journey. This journey is inward out. Then, they start to share their experiences with their fellow beings. They have reached their highest state of consciousness more than once in their life. Some dwell in their higher consciousness all the time, disconnected externally and connected within.

It is very important to know that one who thinks that he is connected to his core goes deeper into his own consciousness and is hesitant in sharing it with the outside world.

People who actually go on this journey march with their own inner self and become one with their soul energy. They feel that they don't want to share the experience with the outside world.

What happens in that case is you are depleted of the total experience and the power that comes with it.

If you decide not to share your journey and the experience, the power that you get from the source energy will get depleted; it begins to diminish.

It is very typical that this powerful energy becomes more powerful only when you share it around. You need to understand that once your consciousness is raised, it will be visible to the world. Why then not share it with others and grow your own self?

The more you give to the world outside, the more you will raise your own consciousness. Actually, it turns out that your soul starts to shine its radiance in you.

You start feeling and relating to experiences. When you feel, see, or just hear the gentle breeze that touches you, your consciousness sends the feeling to your subconscious which in turn connects to your super-subconsciousness. A feeling of oneness and complete union is experienced. Here is oneness with universal energies. Then you start sharing your experiences with the people around you. You help those who are seeking enlightenment, or you just simply help people in order to make this world a better place to live in.

When you start sharing your core energy, your own energy starts to multiply, thus raising your consciousness to the highest point.

The more you give, the more you get.

TASKS

EVERY TASK SHOULD BE CONTINUED WITHOUT FAIL FOR AT LEAST THIRTEEN DAYS IN ORDER TO START SEEING VISIBLE CHANGES IN YOU.

1. Tell yourself every day that you love yourself, and you are grateful to be alive.

2. You are grateful to every part of your body. You can affirm this by saying each part, for example: I thank my legs for carrying my weight every day and not failing me. I thank my heart for pumping blood in my body and giving me life. I thank my eyes for making me see the beautiful world around me.

3. It is very important to remember that these tasks are working magic inside of you hence, gratitude to each part of your physicality is very important.

4. You are grateful to your parents, mother, and father; express this gratitude to them every day. It's important to continue these tasks for a minimum of twenty-one days.

5. Express gratitude to your mother, since she held you for nine months upside-down in that ball of fire. She gave you food and energy even before you opened your eyes.

6. You need to express gratitude to your siblings, friends, and co-workers who define the relationships around you.

7. Every single day, be conscious of saying thank you to at least one person.

8. Begin with your wife, husband, son, daughter, and colleague.

9. Add at least one more "I love you." Be careful in choosing who you start saying this to.

10. It may not be important for you to mention to a stranger, "I love you." Instead, you could mention, "I love the way you drove the bus today," or "I appreciate that you cleaned the garbage from the pantry."

11. This is very, very important: you must consciously express gratitude to at least one person outside of your circle every single day.

12. If you remember just before going to bed that you have not expressed your gratitude to one person today, then pick up your phone, call your friend, and tell him that you appreciate his support in your life. (Now it should not happen every day that you forget to express gratitude to even one single person in your entire day.)

13. Start feeling alive. Be conscious of your breath.

14. Express gratitude to every person in your life.

15. Experience every experience.

PART III

The New You

Spirituality is like the ocean, and religion is like the rivers. The rivers go and merge into the oceans; the ocean does not merge anywhere.

In today's world, unfortunately, people and groups have completely distorted the meaning of the two.

There are so many fights and differences of opinion between various religious groups or within a particular sect, claiming their ownership of God.

Each group criticizes the other, claims their ownership of "their God," and goes to any extent to show the others down.

Why don't countries or groups fight amongst themselves for the name of the Pacific Ocean, or for that matter the sun? Why don't countries or groups say, "The sun is ours; you go find another sun for your group."

Even if the sun is called by different names in different languages the world over, no country or group gets up and says the sun is ours. We all have ownership of it. We don't call the Pacific Ocean by any other name other than the Pacific Ocean!

Then why do we divide God?

The same God is present in each one of us. Why don't we understand that and connect over this, instead of fighting among ourselves?

The simple reason, I believe, is that debating about God gives these groups or people power.

The common man does not understand God and is very vulnerable to buying any explanation given to him. The poor man is already struggling to make ends meet; he has no time to debate about God. He keeps his belief system simple and clean.

Is it not then our duty to help him connect with his own self, the God inside of him, or rather give him a more confusing notion?

It is important to understand that egotism dominates the outside journey and it wants you to be famous between this world and the celestial world: "Everyone should look upon me — no one should be ahead of me." Egotism drives you to say anything and everything to become famous whether this be lies, exaggeration, pointing fingers, or showing others down.

However, the inside journey is one of surrender, and being humble to the point off being crushed, like the henna leaves — they are crushed to make a thin paste. Applied on the hands and feet of brides, only then it gives a beautiful red color.

This is why alone time is very important. When you are alone in silence, you see yourself — and trust me, you don't like what you see.

All the bad ideas in your mind have to be replaced by good ideas.

I would like to give a very basic example here to make it easy to understand.

Have you ever noticed that animals like dogs, cats, and turtles always give birth or lay their eggs in isolation? They don't give birth in the open. Similarly, birds make their nests in the thickest part of the tree.

In human beings, the woman (even in the olden times) gave birth in seclusion/alone, not in public. She does not deliver in front of anyone, as that can create a doubt in her own mind about whether she would be able to really deliver her baby or not.

It is the same within yourself. When you have to give birth to a new you, you need seclusion. You need your own time with yourself.

All the Bad has to be replaced by the Good. This is possible only in solitude, or seclusion, as there has to be no scope of any doubts whatsoever, neither from others nor your own self.

All your doubts have to be replaced with faith in yourself and the God inside of you.

This section teaches you how to give birth to a new you.

10

Transmutation

Take a moment and see how far you have evolved.

Compare yourself with the rose. When the bud appears, it may be part of a bunch or a single one on the stem. It looks beautiful. The planter or the gardener anxiously waits for it to bloom. The plant takes nourishment from the soil. Bright sunshine adds to the glory of its blossom.

When we are growing, we take all kinds of feelings and emotions from the people we are associated with. This is our journey in the outside world.

Now, like us, this rosebud typically has two journeys. One is the connection with the outside world of stem, branch, and plant. For us, this journey is the connection with family, friends, associates, work, food, and exercise.

And there is an internal journey... to bloom inward out.

Just as the rose grows from the inside out, your consciousness also grows from within you, and it becomes visible to the people around you when it is fully bloomed, just like the rose flower.

For you this journey involves connecting within yourself and moving from the conscious to the subconscious, and then to the super-sub-subconscious, until finally merging with the core of your being, which is the soul.

For the rose, the pollen is in the innermost part of the full bloom flower from where the bees gather nectar to make honey.

Have you ever heard that the bee takes the juice from the green part of the flower or while it is still a bud? No?

The final nectar of life or what I call purpose, the real pleasure of being one with the source or simply merging with the source energy, is when the real journey begins.

Until the flower blooms, it is only waiting and moving towards a phase of total surrender that comes in when it is fully bloomed.

For the mind, it is important to open layer-by-layer and finally come to the innermost part — the peaceful light. This is the place where the energy is the most powerful — the core. Once your consciousness has merged with the soul, you are fully bloomed.

To attain this position, it is very important to "let go" or totally surrender. Now what is this total surrender?

The total surrender trusts the power of the universe to guide you and make sure that you are in a position to merge with that energy ball within.

Once you have touched the innermost core or the ball of energy, it is like fire.

It is a different experience that cannot be explained in words or feelings. Only once you have reached that position, come out, and tried to associate with people around you will you understand what I'm saying.

There is a disconnection with the world around you. You are you, but you are within you, not outside of you. You are there, attached with your relations and associates and things, but you are detached.

There are some very typical signs associated with this. One of them would be that the person says, "I am feeling very hot. Why do I start sweating when I meditate?" It's like some kind of a fireball burning inside of you.

It is at this stage that the opening of your chakras becomes very important. The seven chakras that you have within you have the right flow of actinic forces going within your body at this stage.

Here, you become an instrument or a mere medium through which the energy travels from the universe, from your crown chakra to your Muladhara and down to the Earth. Once your chakras are open, the actinic forces start moving and rotating and resonating within your own body. This leads to hot flashes or to some kind of an enlightenment, an awakening, or a position when you start relating yourself to nature and the outside world on a different paradigm altogether. You are at the highest level of your consciousness.

Needless to say, the opening of the chakras is again a very important part of the process of your internal journey. The physical body has to experience these inward experiences of the energy flow. I write in detail about the chakras and the process of opening and healing them in the next book.

At times this resonance of the actinic forces can be so powerful that your entire body starts to resonate. You will feel the palpitation in your entire body.

Instead of feeling the heartbeat only in your chest, you start feeling your heart beating throughout your entire body, through all your chakras. This is an indication that all your chakras are open and the actinic forces are flowing to and fro throughout your body.

At this stage there are typically changes of the elements of your body from one being into the other. These changes indicate a total conversion or transformation of your inner self into a new you. This new you is a seeker and wants to share your newly found wisdom with the rest of the world.

You are the same individual, but your thought processes, your way of looking at things, and your way of understanding your surroundings have all undergone a paradigm shift. You are more sensitive now to the slightest observation around you. This is a new you wherein only you are in a position to first and foremost understand that you have transitioned into a purposeful being who is aware and sensitive to your surroundings. You have raised your consciousness.

There is a shift in the association of people and the way you meet and greet people. There is a change in your physicality because now you have become more vibrant. You are actually a medium, carrying that energy which is now resonating with the universe.

This is a completely new experience of a new you.

Your own inner voice is your best advisor.
It knows you as no one else does. Listen
to it; connect with it.

TASKS

EVERY TASK SHOULD BE CONTINUED
WITHOUT FAIL FOR AT LEAST
THIRTEEN DAYS IN ORDER TO START
SEEING VISIBLE CHANGES IN YOU.

1. Along with the previous tasks, you need to start some serious work now.
2. Start exercising, practicing yoga, or engaging in any kind of physical activity.
3. You need to now follow any kind of discipline. This could be as simple as "I will not eat anything after seven p.m. every day," or "I will regularly attend church service every Sunday."
4. Discipline now is the key.
5. Do not get complacent about seeing the changes in yourself. Instead, connect with yourself.
6. Do one kind thing every day in order to become a better person.

CHAPTER

11

Intellect And Wisdom

The best decision comes to you when you hold the consciousness of your mind's eternity and go with the flow.

Go within yourself for the answers. The best rule in making a decision is when in doubt, do nothing until the subject matter comes so clearly in your mind, so well thought out, that soon the answers will be self-evident to you.

Now you will say, "How can I just do nothing when I am in doubt?" You need to understand that anything you will do at this point will only make you anxious, aggressive, irritated, and start doubting yourself.

Doubt is your biggest enemy, especially if you doubt your own self. In doing so, you doubt the Creator who has created you.

You have to decide what your highest priorities are at this stage. Be honest and trust the transition that you are going through. If you don't trust your own self, how can you make others trust you?

Remember that the enemy of the best is often the good.

Always remember that you are imperfect to the extent that you are the most perfect being there is. There never was, nor shall there ever be, anyone else like you in this universe. So, if you are a masterpiece, then how can you doubt a masterpiece?

These answers that you are seeking will come to you at the right moment: not early, not late. And these answers shall be in conjunction with the energy in the universe and your inner journey, the soul journey.

The universe spins the web for each one of us so that the only way to seek yourself is by going within your own self. There is no other way to go.

Good, positive decisions bring in good, positive actions and thus create positive reactions.

As discussed earlier, your instinctive mind, meaning your rationale, is the one making most of the decisions for you. Now, this intellectual area of your mind bases its decision on knowledge, experience, and practicality, such as this is good for you and this is not good for you. There will be a reason behind this intellectual mind making you do any action. You may not be totally sure of yourself.

However, if you make a decision that is different from what you would have made in that eternity of the moment, then you make it through the intuitive area of the mind or that area which is aware of the real journey of your life.

You are not totally sure of yourself; you do not have enough information to make a good positive decision. Yet the decision you make for yourself at that moment is connected to your innermost self. So here the thought goes from your conscious to your subconscious into your super-subconscious, and then your intuition guides you to do this. No matter what that is, it's your way forward.

Each decision is the foundation of the next series of experiences.

The next set of experiences you go through are always based on your decisions. Now to eat food or drink wine, your intuition is not going to guide you, but to go for a monk's ten-day life cleansing, yes, your inner being is asking you to go for it. It is consciously making you do things. Remember the inward out.

Then you need to go in for your intuitive guidance. As I always say, talk to yourself and listen to yourself; no one knows you better than you.

As a result of this awareness and conjunction between the inner being and you, you become your own master and guide in anything and everything that you want to do.

Everything you communicate to the outside world should come from within your own innermost self. No one knows it better than you, yourself. Your own super-conscious being decides the next set of experimental patterns for you until you ultimately reach a point of complete submission or merging with that ball of energy which this universe is made of.

There is a pattern to reach this place. It's like how all the students studying at Harvard have first completed their primary and secondary grades at different institutions across the world, then they do their undergraduate studies, and finally they come to Harvard.

Similarly, people who are transcendent in life congregate after following the patterns.

Let's discuss each of the stages or transitions wherein you will understand the patterns more clearly.

Step 1: Awareness

Understand that there is a journey and a path. This path is nothing but the road for every being to come from the energy and merge back into the energy. This is the real purpose of life.

Step 2: Observation

As your individual awareness grows and makes you conscious of this journey, you detach from the rational and start observing things from the perspective of purpose. You are now more alive and have the power to observe patterns.

This universe has a strange way of guiding you. It starts showing you patterns. These patterns are in fact guidelines for a lifestyle.

Messages become more and more clear to you.

Now this could take several lifetimes, or in this lifespan only you may come to a point where there is a clear-cut differentiation between the positive master area of the mind and the normal mind that usually stays confused.

THEN YOU COME TO A STATE WHERE YOUR PERCEPTIONS BECOME PRECISE.

Now, once you start making decisions from the up-down way, or the in-out way, they are connected right to the master area guided by the actinic forces running like energy through your body. These decisions come from your super-subconscious to your subconscious and then to your conscious, and that is when you make these decisions.

Typically, it is an inward out journey.

Step 3: Perception

At this stage, your perspective is changed. You start integrating with the forces around you, and you start to connect more with nature. You see yourself as an immortal being revoked and recreated consistently. Day by day, year by year, every transition pattern is making you more evolved. Decisions become easier. Life is more fulfilling and complete.

Oneness with the inner consciousness is experienced. This brings you to a position of bliss.

The soul body begins to merge with the physical body.

Step 4: Metamorphosis

First, the self observes changes in personality followed by the people around you. You start to undergo lifestyle changes and have a completely different perspective to your existence. Inward beauty starts to show radiance in your persona.

Discipline and meditation become a strict ritual every day. The energy becomes so powerful that you start feeling a kind of a pull every time you sit down to meditate. Each meditation becomes more profound than the previous one.

This is the state where the elements of the instinct and the elements of the intellect become one, leading to the supreme life. The instinct is now beginning to transcend and transmute these energies into the immortal body of the soul. The forces are radiating and moving inside out. The consciousness of "the self" is awakening.

This is like when you start a car, and the engine sends the transmitters in action in order to drive the car.

Step 5: Affectionate Detachment

You come into a state of affectionate detachment.

What I mean by affectionate detachment is that you absorb all the powers of the spiritual world within you. When you absorb the spiritual forces or the powers within yourself, you will feel them vibrating through every cell of your body. These forces flow quietly to your most sacral nerves, quieting the mind and bringing the mind into effortless concentration. At this stage you belong more within yourself and less outside of yourself. Now once you feel this attachment with your own inner source energy, you are brought to a place of affectionate detachment.

You are attached to yourself (in the most selfless way) and detached from the outside world. However, this does not mean that you don't love your family, or that you stop doing your daily chores (as mentioned earlier). Instead, you are detached from them in an affectionate manner wherein love is unconditional and just overflowing. Love is sensitive and affectionate but unconditional.

Affectionate detachment is stronger than attachment.

Attachment has questions, fears, and apprehensions (Chapter 1) attached to it. Attachment comes only with questions, not answers. These questions may arise at every stage of your life. You may find answers or you may not. At times, these questions can lead to anxieties and uncertainties; it is then that you need to understand and find your own clarity. It is like the salt and pepper of your life, like the boulders and tree trunks that come in the way of the free-flowing river.

Fear gives rise to attachment.

To be affectionately detached is power, and this power is wisdom.

This wisdom is love that is greater than any emotional love.

Love is born out of understanding. Love merges you into the River of Life and allows the actinic forces to flow within you so that you realize God.

TASKS

EVERY TASK SHOULD BE CONTINUED WITHOUT FAIL FOR AT LEAST THIRTEEN DAYS IN ORDER TO START SEEING VISIBLE CHANGES IN YOU.

Along with all the other tasks, you need to add just 1 very important task.

1. Be honest with yourself.
2. See and observe every single day what you do. Every action should be justified by you, to you.

CHAPTER

12

Detachment In Attachment

Now I am by no means saying, that we leave everything to become a Sanyasi, wandering the jungles in search of peace and solace.

We still have those little attachments of love, care, concern, acceptance, and security. However, now they form a positive aspect of the subconscious mind, as now you are aware of this emotion of love. You become aware of the strings attached to all the worldly, personal, professional, and materialistic things. This does not mean that you stop working, or that you stop loving your family. It is just that you are now becoming aware of the fact that you are born alone and you will die alone, so the sooner you start getting detached, the easier your journey of life will become. Less expectations give you peace now.

Now the subconscious becomes a powerhouse where all negative attachments give birth to positive focus. You have a new eye to see all relationships, events, and in fact the entire world around you.

At first, people may not understand, but gradually, as you exhibit traits, they should. So those who accept these changes in you are there to stay in your life, and those who don't, well, actually, too bad for them. Despite the big boulders in its way, the river does not show resistance. Perhaps the river takes the boulders with it into the sea.

Have you ever seen a mighty river gushing down the mountains, tormenting its way through? It is relentless, cruel, and brutal, taking anything and everything coming in its way. It is powerful to the extent that if nurtured well, one could generate electricity.

That is the power of this energy flow inside of you.

You are torrid, aware of the energy that you carry within you, but at the same time you are sensitive to the people around you.

You are more within yourself, and less with the outside world.

Now this newly found cultivated, affectionate detachment gives you a feeling of belongingness to your surroundings and people. You experience a new feeling of empathy and attachment with your people and loved ones. Most importantly, you have a feeling of completion, a feeling of satisfaction, and a feeling of bliss.

Let go of the past; let go of the future; let go of anything that is around you.

To be alive is being right now in this moment.

Being detached does not mean running away or being insensitive.

Instead, detachment makes you more aware, more giving, more sensitive, more friendly, more human, and closer to family and friends.

Now, by practicing affectionate detachment you are learning to live in the here and now, this moment.

You are awakening the power of direct cognition, which enables you to understand what happens, when it happens, and why it happens.

You are turning into the great river with its authentic flow which is first visible on its surface. You must turn this energy into teachings in order to give you that wisdom.

Not everyone around you will understand you. They should be able to become aware of the fact that you are on a different path altogether.

This is when you are ready to fly.

Inner consciousness has now brought you to a place of no return. Your intellect and wisdom have aligned to become one.

You are in the same world, but you are outside of it. You are a part of it, but you are detached from it. You are alive and conscious of your own journey now. You are taking time for your old spiritual enfoldment.

It is important to understand that this is a state of mind. This intellect gives you a sense of responsibility to feel the change and be a part of it. This should just be a transitory stage; you are not going to be sitting at this level forever.

Most people who begin meditation and glimpse the light feel that this is the ultimate level, and they tend to stay.

No, this is just the mirage effect of the light that you are seeing. This is just a trailer. Trust me, the real light is mesmerizing.

This is a very crucial and vulnerable state, as the more time you take to understand this light, the less pleasure you will have. The greater your awareness and meditation, the faster you will attain permanent enlightenment.

This is the stage where service to mankind will help you to transition faster. Be aware, be kind, do right, become selfless.

Selfless service to mankind makes you free from bondage in this world of mortals.

Your service to mankind begins with your family (as discussed earlier) and then radiates out to the world.

As you progress, your intuition starts walking faster than its rational since your mastermind becomes more active.

You may use spontaneity to connect, and then you will observe that intuition and logic are one.

For example, you might just feel like calling your mother who is thousands of miles away, and it turns out that she has a fever.

Another time you may want to pray and heal your ailing father, who is sitting miles away. Your super-consciousness connected you to your master mind and gave you an intuition that was spontaneous. You called and checked his health, meditated, healed him, and then came back to your own rational being in the Now. Those of you who have experienced this will completely understand what I am saying here. Your intuition becomes very strong.

At this stage, you might also have out-of-body experiences. Now that is a different transition altogether and it is very profound.

As you raise your consciousness, you can start feeling out-of-body experiences. In order to understand and tap your energy at this stage, you will need a proper guide. You may go to experience the connectivity but may not be able to come back to your rational being right now. Or you may experience it just for a second. These experiences should be discussed with your guru or mentor in order to understand the direction in which you need to go further.

As your consciousness arises, it starts becoming very powerful.

When you start experiencing these kinds of outbursts, a few people will start saying that you have become psychic.

My husband and my son would always blame me by saying, "You said it, so it happened."

Initially even I did not realize it, but now I do. It is not that I say it so it happens. Instead, I feel what is happening and what is going to happen. Today, I can still see what is to come.

Again, actions lead you to the path of super-consciousness where you are the final decision. You are the master because the master is in you.

At this stage you are aware of the fact that you and the master are now one.

Now the energies flowing in you go deeper and deeper in, and in, and more in. Your metaphysical and philosophical sides become one. You will begin to realize small patches where energy flows.

Suddenly, the intuitive mind becomes more powerful. Your predictions are on point to the extent that the subconscious will have more than it can handle of the inner teachings. It takes a while for the conscious mind to be convinced that you are a spiritual being whose existence does not begin or end with this life. This inner teaching needs to be applied as soon as it is felt.

You are now an energy bomb. You need to become aware of this energy and keep this energy in you.

Silence is bliss.

You tend to stay quieter now. You are more connected with the inside than to the outside.

It is interesting to mention here that when you first start experiencing the gush of super-consciousness, you tend to talk, talk, and talk. You share the slightest of things with the people around you. People feel you have gone crazy.

You may be physically present in a place with your loved ones around you, but spiritually or internally you will be connected with your own source and probably transitioning into a different zone of meditation altogether. It's interesting that you have the gush of the superpower, the outflow of the energy that you are just beginning to experience. Suddenly you will tend to become quieter. While earlier you would jump at the slightest thing, today you are no longer affected. It's not that you have become insensitive; rather, you are more sensitive. You are meditating on the solution internally. You are no longer vocal about it.

This new you just wants to sit in silence and feel. When you were trying to tell everyone what your intuitions were telling you, they were all against you, they didn't believe you, they did not understand you, and they did not relate to you.

Today, you are so much in yourself that your own intuitions, your own predicaments, and your own predictions are coming through.

Your psychic side is much stronger than your open side. You are quiet; you speak fewer words. Everyone finds it strange, but the less you speak, the more they feel and understand that you are blessed.

TASKS

EVERY TASK SHOULD BE CONTINUED WITHOUT FAIL FOR AT LEAST THIRTEEN DAYS IN ORDER TO START SEEING VISIBLE CHANGES IN YOU.

1. All your tasks now should be involuntary.
2. You should not need to push yourself to do these tasks.
3. Practice discipline, love everyone, care for everyone.
4. Consciously feel no anger or resentment.
5. Forgive yourself every day. This could be as simple as, "I forgive myself for all the wrongs done by me, or by anyone to me."
6. Forgive one person every day who you feel has done anything wrong to you.
7. If the hatred is so grievous, then ask the superpowers for forgiveness. This could be as simple as, "Dear God, please forgive those who hate me. Please forgive me for being biased and having a feeling of hatred against…" (You are free to use names and make your task specific.)
8. Start meditations every morning or evening. Initially join a meditation center to understand how to do the practice, and then start meditating alone.

13

The Super-Conscious Mind

The super-conscious mind is the most wonderful area of the mind.

However, awareness is not always in the mind. You do not always live in this section of the mind. Also, you are not always conscious in the super-conscious mind. You are generally aware in the conscious mind, and you may be visiting your own subconscious mind now and then. In your meditations you should be able to connect with your super-subconscious mind.

However, to reach your super-conscious mind is the entire game. You are consciously living within your super-subconscious mind. You are physically in the Now, but in your consciousness you are one with the One.

The more and more you detach, your own awareness of the conscious mind arises and the conscious mind attaches itself with the super-subconscious mind.

You become more super-conscious.

You tend to feel as if you are completely living in the moment, as if there is no past and there is no future. You are subconsciously certain that you are now becoming intense vibrating entities of the eternal. And this is very real, as real as a table, pen, or chair. This is super-consciousness.

When your awareness is in super-consciousness, you see yourself as a pure life force. You become aware of the same energy flowing through people, fruit, trees, and everything.

I have felt this myself during my meditation as flowing and gliding over the oceans, flying in the sky with no wings.

Super-consciousness is so permanent, so surreal, that nothing could touch it and nothing could hurt it. In this state you see the external world like a dream. Things begin to look transparent. People become transparent. At times people confuse this higher level of consciousness with out-of-body experience. But these are completely different things.

In out-of-body experience, you travel out of your body in your consciousness to be somewhere else, and then you come back into your own consciousness. However, living in your super-consciousness is being alive, very sensitive and aware within your own consciousness and your own body. Here you may be connected to your own super-consciousness while being detached from people around you.

This is a very beautiful and natural state to be in. While you are looking at another person, you are suddenly penetrating into his mind, his thoughts, and what he is thinking at that particular moment of time. Everything is crystal clear. He stands completely transparent in front of you and your X-ray eyes. Your super-consciousness is now connecting with his consciousness; hence, you are able to read him.

This super-consciousness brings a different kind of a feeling of belongingness to the extent that you want to go out and help people who are seeking a similar path. You feel like a grade twelve high school student who can help junior school children to follow the same path.

Note that the path into the tunnel is the same for everyone. What is important is how you reach the tunnel.

The tunnel is the state where you start dwelling in your super-conscious mind. Your entire existence of your life is only in the zone called super-consciousness. Physically, you are aware and dilated outside; but internally, you are connected. It's like flying over the mountains and over the ocean because all the energy of the universe connects to your super-consciousness and makes you feel alive.

TASKS

EVERY TASK SHOULD BE CONTINUED
WITHOUT FAIL FOR AT LEAST
THIRTEEN DAYS IN ORDER TO START
SEEING VISIBLE CHANGES IN YOU.

Follow all your tasks diligently.

1. Read your journal from day one and see if you have missed out on anything.
2. By now, the changes in you should be visible.
3. Meditation time should be your time alone with yourself.
4. You should start looking forward to your daily meditation time.

CHAPTER

14

Affirmation

You need to understand the power of affirmation.

What is affirmation?

I am repeatedly showing my firm "intent" that "I can" confirm and reconfirm to first my consciousness and then into my subconsciousness and then to my super-consciousness that "I can and I will."

Up until now, you have gained a little insight into this journey called life. Now it's important to know what will be your driving force. There is no set path. There is no GPS that will take you to your destination, so how are you going to work this through?

You have to first strongly believe in what you can do before you even jump into this.

The bond of commitment is to your own self.

Once you confirm and commit to yourself, you will need to give yourself and your consciousness this constant dose of confirmation. This is a lifelong relationship with yourself. At every step you need to affirm your consciousness so that it reaches your subconsciousness and your super-subconsciousness.

You will notice that some days the meditation is perfect and other days you just don't connect. The latter are way more frequent than the former, but this does not mean that you do not have to affirm yourself. You need to affirm yourself every minute of the day, every day of the month, and every year in your life, and this is what the journey is all about.

Now, in order to affirm your new life and thoughts, you must start to remold your ideas and thoughts. You are the one who knows best what you want in this life of yours, so start remolding the ideas to a new you in your affirmations. First make a conscious decision about your affirmations. Once you become conscious of what you are affirming, your conscious mind will send signals to your subconscious mind so that it starts creating an impression on your day-to-day life of confirming your affirmation.

Your awareness grows.

When used on this inward journey, affirmation is actually wisdom for spiritual reasons. Affirmation is a power which can be understood only through meditation.

Now you cannot just go on an affirmation spree. Before you begin to work on affirmation, you must understand completely from within what you are doing.

Make sure that when your subconsciousness has been remolded you can take the added responsibilities, the new adventures, and the challenges that will manifest as a result of breaking out of one force field and entering into another.

Now, on a very serious note, you need to prepare yourself physically and mentally before even thinking of entering into this commitment.

Once determined, there's no looking back. You are going ahead to be a part of the cosmic energy which is a life force not only on this planet but in the universe at large.

Only when you are fully ready and prepared to accept the new effect of your efforts should you proceed with any affirmation.

When learning to drive, you need to first get your learner's license and then move on to your professional license. It is best to get permission from the authorities before you start driving on the highways. Similarly, before committing to affirmation, it is very important for you to understand the consequences of the affirmation. It is important to mentally and physically prepare yourself to accept the energy that will come with the affirmation that you make and decide.

The affirmations you make can be very powerful. The power that comes with these affirmations is raw power. By power, I mean it is a rich energy that will envelop you. You can use this energy in any possible way that you want to. It is like placing a loaded AK-47 in the hands of a man. If the man doesn't know the power of it, he could destroy everything around him; and if he knows when and where to use it, well…

All I am trying to say here is that affirmation is serious business.

An affirmation is a series of positive words repeated time and time again with a visual concept attached to it. This visual concept needs to be either the place you want to reach through your affirmation, or the connection with the higher forces that you chant upon.

Such a statement can be repeated mentally or better verbally since words alone without a picture frame shall have no meaning.

When you are affirming a quotation, it is important for you to visualize it in your consciousness. Transmitting it to your subconsciousness will then allow you to conceptualize an image and an aura picture of power to which you are surrendering.

In the affirmation, you commit yourself in gratitude to the power force.

Affirmation basically helps you to connect with the energy of the universe so that the universe starts making things happen for you. But the bottom line here is that the connection of your subconscious mind with the universe is the image personified by your super-subconscious mind.

So, a real clear picture in your affirmation meditation should be visible to you for you to surrender in complete salutation.

Remember that whatever you are asking for, you need to be prepared to take charge and be responsible for it.

Remember that everything and every force has its consequences.

How to decide what you want to affirm is the most crucial thing. You need to be very consciously aware of the fruition of your affirmation. Thus, you need to seriously think about what you want to manifest.

For example, every day you affirm to yourself that you will become financially independent before the end of this year. Consciously, every single day you affirm and strive towards your goal. Visible signs of fruition of your affirmation should be seen in six to eight weeks. You should continue your affirmation; in fact, you can make it stronger by adding more specifications. For example, you could affirm, "Along with becoming financially independent, I will also become debt-free before the end of the year."

Here are some simple steps toward making the right affirmation:

Step 1: You begin by understanding what you do not need in your life.

Typically, affirmation is asking the universe to bless you with something, so how can you ask for something that you do not need?

It's as simple as that.

Step 2: You become aware of the things you want in your life.

Step 3: Start taking steps to change the things that you do not want.

It's simple. You must first get rid of old furniture before you go out to buy new furniture.

Step 4: Start making room for the new consciousness that will come along with your affirmation.

Now whether one is dealing with furniture, thoughts, concepts, self-created inhibitions, or doubts, these act as blocks and barriers. For the subconscious mind, they act like boulders that you need to clear up.

Step 5: Simply de-clutter, whether it's your external surroundings or your internal thoughts and inhibitions. Just clean your surroundings as well as your mind.

Step 6: Commit.

Here commitment is not just one hundred percent; it has to be one thousand percent or maybe more. You have to replace "I can't" with "I will" and "I have to," no matter what.

Now the moment your consciousness is determined, your super-consciousness will send you surges of energy and strength to affirm and reaffirm.

Have you ever seen an ant climb up a wall carrying just one grain of sugar? It falls down half way, then again it picks up the grain and start climbing up. It falls back down again and again… until it finally reaches the top of the wall.

You need to affirm fifty, one hundred, or five hundred times until you start relating to your affirmation. Make your affirmation so firm that even if consciously you are not chanting it, your subconscious mind will continue the chant.

Your affirmation has to get embodied in you, in your bloodstream, until it reaches your soul. It is then that your raised consciousness will work with the universal energies to confirm and bless your affirmation.

Now as I said earlier, this is not easy. You will have resisting thoughts. You will not like to do your routine, etc.

Here you need to fully understand that as your vibrations rise, forces will come to work against your raised consciousness. You will face resistance, like the boulders. People and forces transcending at lower frequencies are afraid of awakening the spiritual powers. They are afraid of you. They do not want you to lift your own vibrations.

People who believe in doing black magic or tantric prayers in order to create boulders or obstructions for others actually end up paying a very heavy price.

At this stage, if you go to someone who is not vibrating higher than you, they might end up misguiding you since they themselves are struggling.

Here you need to fully trust your own energy, the universe, and most importantly your own faith in your own self.

You need to be aware of the master in you, and you need to believe that everything is for your good only.

By no means am I saying, don't go to the yogis or other people who claim to be "evolved." All I am saying is that if they were so evolved themselves, then they should have done good for themselves, too, shouldn't they?

You need to understand that failure doesn't matter to you. You need to keep going on.

Relentless.

Whenever you feel low or weak, remember the ant. Once affirmed, giving up is not a solution.

Tell yourself you can and you will.

If you have come this far, you cannot let it go now.

There will be moments of self-doubt which will pull you away from your affirmation. This is what you need to overcome until you start feeling the power of the affirmation on you.

You are experiencing a complete reprogramming of your consciousness, both internally and externally.

The passive forces of your internal consciousness that were dormant until now are taking charge and becoming more aggressive and visible, but in the most positive way for you.

It is like cleaning a dusty mirror. When you wipe it with Lysol and rub it repeatedly, it becomes crystal clear to the extent that you don't even feel that there is glass. You can clearly see through it.

Your determined affirmation makes your path clean and clear and your vision transparent, spotless. You are being guided by your super-subconsciousness now, which is giving you the vision, showing you the path. You are in a situation where you can acquire what you need: most importantly, happiness.

"I Am The Complete Master Of All My Forces."

"I am totally in control of what is happening in and around my world. My higher energies and connection are holding and leading me through."

You must understand that affirmation gives you "power of awareness." By this I mean that affirmation consciously and unconsciously forces you to live in the moment. *Subconsciously, when you affirm you are aware of your affirmation.*

So, you come to a point where

You Are Exactly Who You "Will" To Be – And You Will Be Exactly Who You Intend To Be - A Masterpiece.

TASKS

EVERY TASK SHOULD BE CONTINUED
WITHOUT FAIL FOR AT LEAST
THIRTEEN DAYS IN ORDER TO START
SEEING VISIBLE CHANGES IN YOU.

After reading this far, you understand the meaning and importance of these tasks.

1. Repeat your affirmations more than thirty times.
2. Every time you see something beautiful, connect with it.
3. It could be as simple as taking a moment at the stop sign. Just observe the clouds in the sky, or a simple sparrow sitting by the corner of the pavement.
4. Now start to affirm what you want from the universe.
5. Be careful; it should be a very clear blessing. Affirm that you are ready to face the consequences of it in full.
6. Your meditation should be done religiously every day.
7. Respect yourself, people around you, and your existence at large.

15

Highest High
And Lowest Low

In a few days, you will see that your affirmation will start working a new chemistry within you. Your subconscious forces start moving you towards your affirmation. The universe starts sending you signals everywhere.

You find yourself on a different platform.

Now this is not as simple as it sounds.

It takes determination like the ant's earnest desire to be successful even if you fail again and again. There are so many people who just give up when they do not see anything coming.

Understand that the light at the end of the tunnel is not an illusion; the tunnel is.

The light is your own reflection, and the tunnel is how simple or complicated you want to make this "life."

So, as mentioned earlier, it's your own perception.

Often when you feel things do not go your way, you experience a challenge or defeat, or during any situation that is testing your nerves, it's actually a stage of evolution in your own journey.

For example, have you ever sat in a roller coaster?

When you are waiting in line for your turn, your excitement is the highest and the fear is the lowest. As you sit down and buckle up, you are excited about what you will be experiencing.

Now slowly and gradually the rollercoaster climbs up to the point where you can't see anything below. At this point your excitement is at its lowest and your fear is its highest.

With butterflies in your stomach, you are apprehensive and nervous. You pray to get out of this safely. And lo and behold, as the rollercoaster comes down, you swing between feeling nervous, excited, and scared — all emotions at once. You feel that it's the end of life.

When the ride comes to a stop, you breathe a sigh of relief.

Understand that your highest point on that roller coaster was your lowest point of confidence and self-belief.

And when you came down and stepped off of the ride, you were at the highest point of confidence and self-belief.

So typically, your highest high point is your lowest low point in self-belief, and your lowest low point is your highest high point.

Those readers who have attended my sessions and are being guided by me will fully understand this. I have explained this to you on your own life journey at the point when you were at your highest high and lowest low.

Now remember the lowest low is actually the bottom where you can fall. It's like complete failure and disownment when you feel the heavens are falling down (actually the heavens never fall down).

This is the moment when you need to connect with your inner self, your core, and your consciousness. This is the moment to feel and recognize who you are and what you intend to be.

This is the moment of a true you.

In your meditations too, there will be moments when you feel totally disconnected, depressed, and as if nothing is happening. Actually, a lot is happening.

The fact that you are experiencing this lowest low point means that you will only go higher and better in your life, provided you believe in yourself and this amazing journey called life.

You and you alone have the capability of changing your life from what it is to where you want to take it. The moment you become aware of your lowest low, you will start to see your highest high.

The strength of your affirmation at this point is being tested. This is the only ship that will sail you to your highest high point, always.

When you recognize this, your affirmations become strong, stronger, and strongest.

Now you want to do this.

Your inner light begins to dawn. The clairvoyance becomes visible to you.

Your affirmations show fruition. You start becoming alive, aware, and cleansed. You feel different.

You feel totally connected with the universe around you. You are more connected with the universe, nature, and its energy than with the people.

You are the light at the end of the tunnel. You are radiant and vibrant. People start to observe these changes in you.

You have successfully touched your innermost core of super-subconsciousness, which is nothing but the light of your being, and that has started illuminating your subconsciousness and consciousness and is now visible to the world.

In Buddhism it is believed that once you come to this stage, you want to detach from the world. If you observe the monks, they believe in retaining this energy by not interacting much with people or the outside world. They speak less often; they lead a disciplined life.

Certainly, discipline is the key to this process.

Now once you are at this point of no return, you can be there, experience detachment in attachment, be aware of your existence, and share with the world, the story of your journey.

The answers to your questions become clear. The things which raised questions in your mind so long ago are now appearing crystal clear.

All mysteries are solved; all questions are answered.

This is the state when you become aware of your consciousness.

The purpose of your life is right in front of you: TO MERGE IN THE LIGHT.

TASKS

EVERY TASK SHOULD BE CONTINUED
WITHOUT FAIL FOR AT LEAST
THIRTEEN DAYS IN ORDER TO START
SEEING VISIBLE CHANGES IN YOU.

1. Try to combine your daily routine of meditation with some kind of chanting.
2. At least once a week, go out in nature to sit and meditate.
3. Consciously by now you should be eating healthy.

CHAPTER

16

Success

Many times, I have been asked, "What is success?"

First of all, let me be clear that the moment you even have this word on your tongue, you started seeing the cloud.

Success is a very relative term, meaning, for example, if you get up at two in the afternoon (yes, some people have the luxury to sleep that late), and at a stretch you are in a position to get up every day at ten a.m., then that is success.

But what happens on the tenth day? Do you again start getting up at two p.m.? Now, once you find yourself a job which requires you to be in your office by nine a.m., lo and behold: the first month is a disaster. You would have perhaps thought three hundred times within those thirty days about quitting your job and going back to bed. And Sundays and holidays are total hibernation. So where is the success? It is more like a forced routine you are not interested in.

Another example is if you can follow a rigid diet plan for a week, is that success?

What happens on the first weekend after your diet regime and you enjoy perhaps the best pasta you have had in ages? On the following Monday, you again get the ball rolling to make sure that you follow the diet religiously.

So, then what is success?

If you return to the point that is exactly from where you started, the net outcome in both the cases is literally returning to the point from where you started.

Isn't it dangerous? Your perception of the mind is that you wanted to do something for a certain period of time and you did it and that's the end of the story.

Success is actually a conscious effort by you.

Consciously set the alarm for seven-thirty a.m. Perhaps set four or five alarms starting at eight a.m. at fifteen-minute intervals so that you make sure that you get up by seven-thirty a.m. every single day in order to reach the office by nine a.m.

Perhaps you can post your diet plan on your fridge, or on your cupboard, or everywhere around the house.

You are not going to have any chocolate. You are not going to resist every temptation of eating chocolate. So, what are you basically doing here?

You are trying to create a pattern which will help you put in the required conscious effort in order to achieve the goal you set for yourself.

Now this pattern becomes so strong that even if your conscious mind tends to forget this pattern, your subconsciousness alerts your consciousness of the pattern.

Then you will succeed in your timely waking up or your diet plan.

Now when people just put in a conscious effort in their workplace, for sure you will get success, but here it is a little different.

Yes, you go to the office every day. You make sure that you reach your office fifteen minutes earlier than John every day. But still, you do not meet your targets.

Mr. A. had one of the most morose faces when he expressed his failure to me: "Also, I make sure that I finish all my pending work or at least try to finish it all during the week. Still, I am ignored."

Many members of the younger generation come to ask me such questions.

In today's society, you need things instantly. You command your phone to track the meaning or pronunciation of Worcestershire sauce, and there you are: the pronunciation with the exact meaning is right there.

Imagine: to understand how to pronounce a word that is a part of your grocery list every month, you instantly ask Siri on your phone.

Success here is instant.

Then why don't you have the instant success when you're working or trying to lose weight or trying to put yourself on a disciplined pattern?

You need to understand that right now I am not talking about the spiritual path; I am simply talking about our day-to-day lives.

All we are discussing is your day-to-day challenges that get extended and bring you to a point where you feel disillusioned and give up hope.

My dear, as the old saying goes, the more sugar you put in the tea, the sweeter it is. That's exactly how simple it is.

To be successful, the most important thing is to understand what you want to succeed in.

Is it pleasing your seniors, or is it just losing ten pounds? Is it changing your lifestyle, or does it refer to changing your life as you reach for higher vibrations?

Notwithstanding the fact that the efforts of Mr. A. are less, or that he does not complete the timesheets every day, there is still some ingredient missing in the success quotient fired by him.

Mr. A. has done everything right, including making a cup of coffee from the machine for his boss in the morning, although very reluctantly. Still, he hasn't been rewarded for his efforts by his boss. What could be the reason?

I do not want to make you feel that, "She is aiming at making me put forth every effort to stay away from my favorite pie and ice cream every week."

Success is not the result of your efforts alone.

All those efforts have to be accompanied by FAITH:

Faith in your own self;

Faith in "I can do it"; and

Faith in "I have to do it."

"I have faith in myself and I can make this happen."

"Faith in the God inside of you. To the One you have to connect and become One ".

The moment this element of faith comes in you, bingo — you are now truly hitting the target bang on.

Now Mr. A. has that hot cup of coffee in his hand for his boss. He gives it to him in the sweetest way possible, like an eligible bachelorette serving a cup of tea to the appropriate groom in front of the entire family.

Come on, this is not matchmaking, my friend. Oh, if you want to succeed in the job you are doing, then impress your boss with that cup of coffee. You are not matchmaking here.

You have to carry this assertiveness with that cup of yours over your shoulders when you enter your boss's room. You have to make him feel that you are the most precious member of his team at that point of time; you are his 'knight' who will get him to achieve his numbers and help him hit his promotion.

You are not the sweet shy bride cooking dinner each night and waiting at the door for his "lordship" to come back.

Now the moment your effort is combined with faith in yourself, success is achieved. Well, at least we are getting the ingredients in place for a delicious recipe called Success.

I have had people ask me, "Why am I so low in self-esteem? I constantly have fears that I will not succeed. I don't think I can make it."

No, I am not going to give you stories of Karma, this is your destiny, you were not meant to do it, etc. etc.

For me, all these are more like excuses we give to ourselves whenever we fail, but I leave them for my spiritual journey and not my promotion.

Your promotion is in your hands. As realistic as the soap bar in your hands every morning.

Similarly, your success is in your hands. It is the quantum of the efforts with sincerity that you put in your task, in all earnestness, while being honest with yourself. You perceive how much, how soon, and how effectively you want to use your own strength and conviction in order to succeed.

Now the moment you have faith in yourself, what are you going to do?

Unconsciously, you are trying to connect to that inner self of yours, which is there, but you ignored it every day.

This inner self will reassure you that you can do it.

I always tell people, "Talk to yourself as much as you can. It may sound strange, but it is the truth."

The only thing that can help you succeed in whatever you do is reassessing your own self before others assess or reassess you.

When I say reassess yourself, it is important for you to understand your goal. Focus on your goal and see how far you are from it. Are you actually on the bus which is leading you to your goal, or have you deviated?

If you are not sure whether you can do this thing or not, will you ever be in a position to do it?

The answer will be no, in any case. Your gut is more aware of you than you are. Your inner self knows you best. There is no one in this world that knows you better than your own inner self.

So, if your inner voice is saying you cannot stick to the diet regime or you cannot lose ten pounds in one month, understand and accept the fact that you need to put in more effort in order to be successful here.

If your inner self is saying no, but there is some part of you that is saying yes, there's no harm in trying. This is something which can be worked on in a positive way using affirmations. Other external tools can help you as well.

For example, if inside of me I know I cannot keep up my diet plan for a month, then would I ever succeed after one week?

In order to succeed, you have to first of all convince your own self that what you are going to do is really good for you. Once you have connected with your consciousness and have decided to go ahead, then all you need to do is put in honesty and due diligence in anything that you want to succeed in.

When you connect internally to your own higher consciousness, your consciousness and your subconsciousness will align to help you achieve results.

Success is guaranteed.

Literally everything is within you.

Go within layers and layers of consciousness to the subconsciousness to the super-sub-subconsciousness in order to merge within.

Now, let us take these examples to our spiritual journey.

As mentioned earlier, the journey is from the inward out. Understand that until you understand your higher consciousness and are realistic in your affirmations, you do not give your own self the honesty and affirmation that you can do it and you will never be able to succeed.

The same principles apply on your spiritual journey. You need to first understand and prepare yourself physically, mentally, and emotionally to go on this journey. Only then can you really understand and start doing or seeing changes within yourself.

This process needs to continue until you have achieved your first few glances of that light. Then you will realize that you are a blessed soul. You do have a journey inside to carry. There is a purpose for your life.

There is a purpose for your existence, which you need to convey to the rest of the world.

Now the power becomes so strong that what you said or felt while doing meditation becomes visible with open eyes.

This is success on your inward journey.

You can perceive the same energy, the same connection.

You come to a state of constant meditation.

In this state, even if you are sitting with other people, anywhere, you are still connected to your own energy levels. You are experiencing detachment in attachment.

As mentioned earlier, this is not a permanent state of mind. You will feel it coming or going.

Success will be when you are in this position or in this day for your entire life, but in order to be in this position, you first need to understand that you have already succeeded, even if it is for a fraction of a second, in your journey.

If you are in a position to come to this point once, then you will have the desire or the urge to come to this position always.

This will need a lot of meditation and discipline.

Once you are permanently in this state where no one can touch you, this is a permanent state. This is your permanent color.

You need to experience this to believe this.

Continued.......

TASKS

EVERY TASK SHOULD BE CONTINUED WITHOUT FAIL FOR AT LEAST THIRTEEN DAYS IN ORDER TO START SEEING VISIBLE CHANGES IN YOU.

1. You should have completed and diligently performed all of the tasks in thirty-nine days. If you failed, start again.
2. Before you start, just ask the superpowers to help and give you strength to be diligent for forty days.
3. Ask your family or friends to join in the cleansing and changing process.
4. Give yourself only forty days to transform yourself into a new you who you did not even know existed.
5. On the fortieth day, be grateful. Be in total gratitude to yourself and the entire universe for making this transformation happen.
6. Gratitude is the key.

www.ingramcontent.com/pod-product-compliance
Lightning Source LLC
Chambersburg PA
CBHW060935050726
47592CB00003B/960